THE CIVIL WAR SOLDIER

The CIVIL WAR SOLDIER

A Photographic Journey

RAY M. CARSON

Foreword by James I. Robertson, Jr.

GRAMERCY BOOKS
NEW YORK

Copyright © 2000 by Stackpole Books

This 2007 edition is published by Gramercy Books, an imprint of Random House Value Publishing, a division of Random House, Inc., New York, by arrangement with Stackpole Books.

Gramercy is a registered trademark and the colophon is a trademark of Random House, Inc.

Random House
New York • Toronto • London • Sydney • Auckland
www.randomhouse.com

Printed and bound in China.

A catalog record for this title is available from the Library of Congress.

ISBN: 978-0-517-22897-5

10 9 8 7 6 5 4 3 2 1

⌇ Contents

Acknowledgments

There are a number of people to thank for making this book possible: my parents, Ray and Mary, for instilling in me a lifelong interest in history; my wife, Renée, for her belief in my work and support on this project; my sons, Mark and Christopher, for giving me an incentive to prove that history is not just dates and numbers, but real people with real stories; fellow writer and Civil War aficionado Diane Fischler, for her insight; and Ann Baird, for her support of my photography by exhibiting my work in her galleries. Lastly, my thanks to the entire Civil War reenacting community for their dedication in accurately portraying the life and times of our ancestors. Without them, this book would not have been possible. Very special thanks to: the 115th New York, Company A; the 48th New York, Company F; the 8th Florida, Company B; the 7th Florida, Company K; the 3rd Florida, Company A; and 1st Stuart Horse Artillery, Pelham's Battery.

⌾ Foreword

The story of the Civil War is really the story of three million young men who got into uniform by a process not all of them quite understood and who hoped that they would somehow live through it to get back home to cherish in old age the great memories of their youth.

Soldiers of blue and gray were ordinary men who made the Civil War a very extraordinary struggle. None of them ever resembled a European-type soldier. Incurably, a Johnny Reb or Billy Yank looked like precisely what he was: a civilian who had put on a uniform and picked up a weapon because there was a job to be done. Yet he never let the uniform, or some smart-talking officer make much difference in either his thinking or his behavior.

Some men enlisted for popular reasons: everybody else was doing it, it seemed like an adventurous and romantic course to take, or because pressure from family and sweetheart was too deep to ignore. Many volunteered to avoid the epithet of coward. Others entered the army because the waving flag or the moving phrases of orators and posters struck a chord of patriotic feeling—some sense of honor that could not be shoved aside.

The greatest tragedy of that tragic war is that both sides were fighting for the same thing: American freedom. To the average Northern soldier, the issue was the preservation of the Union. Beginning in 1863, changing the nature of that union by erasing the word "slavery" from the American language became a second goal in the Northern war effort.

For the average Southern soldier, preserving the government created by the Founding Fathers was paramount. The constitution was not some fluid document adjusting with time. When the other side refused to acknowledge protection of slavery guaranteed by the federal statutes, Southern states left the union to preserve what had been.

A North and a South, each conscious of its superior way, and each convinced of the total evil of the other, went to war in order to defend home and God's interests. One side looked forward, the other backward. Their different interpretation of what America ought to be was the basis of the bloodiest four years in the nation's history.

John Hagan of Georgia made an early observation that could have been said by men on either side. "I believe we will have to fight like Washington did, but I hope our people will never be reduced to destress & poverty as the people of that day was, but if nothing else will give us our liberties I am willing for the time to come."

Élan and naivete sent youths rushing to recruiting offices. Recruits were eager to fight, but few of them knew how. The farmboys and students who enlisted in the armies had no conception of discipline, drill, life in the open, long marches, following orders unhesitatingly, mastering weapons, digging earthworks, and eating unfamiliar food. They faced diseases they had never known and wounds they had never anticipated. Through it all, the men of blue and gray would endure loneliness and homesickness to a degree none of them ever imagined.

Their state of mind is the key to their actions. The average Northern and Southern volunteer was an individualist who never thought of himself as a professional soldier. He was a civilian on loan to the military, and he never let the military interfere too much with his deeply ingrained traits of independence, pride, humor, and fear of God.

Modern communications did not exist in the 1860s. The written word was the basic form of contact. Thousands of soldiers recorded their thoughts and activities in letters, diaries, sketches, histories, and paintings. Their collective output provides an unprecedented record of the common soldier in war.

The majority of Civil War volunteers were in their early twenties, white, Protestant, and unmarried. A soldier of average size was 5 feet 7 inches tall and weighed 135 pounds. David Van Buskirk of the 27th Indiana was an inch short of seven feet. When he wearied of men gawking at him, Van Buskirk would say that at his departure for war, each of his six sisters "leaned down and kessed me on top of my head."

Union encampments tended to contain a babel of tongues. One of every five Billy Yanks was a first-generation American. Germans comprised the largest bloc of immigrants, with Irishmen running a close second. It was not unusual to have in an all-foreign regiment an interpreter to translate outgoing and incoming dispatches. Following the implementation of the Emancipation Proclamation, more than 180,000 blacks added their strength to the ranks of the Federal armies.

The enthusiasm that propelled young men into service quickly turned to wonder, envy, and foreboding once they got to camp. There was so much to learn, so many strange environments to conquer. The widespread presence of sickness and disease shook confidence; and as the idea of battle came closer to reality, fear as often as not replaced bravado.

Meanwhile, for forty-nine of every fifty days, the Civil War soldier was in camp. "Our home was the regiment," Louisianian William Watson noted, "and the farther we got from our native state the more we became attached to it." Yet camp life was unlike anything an eager recruit ever imagined.

Opposing armies tended to tramp back and forth across the same ground. Encampments regularly occurred where bivouacs had been. The area was unsanitary, the region barren. In the summer, a Union artilleryman observed capriciously, "a grasshopper could jump and it would create such a cloud of dust that Confederates thought the army was on the move."

Wet weather was no improvement. Soldiers often likened their camps to a swamp, quagmire, or "wallow hole." Following a week of rain, a Virginia soldier called his encampment "a lake of mud" with ground "so soft that you have to hold your breath to keep from sinking." A visitor to the area, he added, would be perplexed whether to laugh or sympathize."

A normal day in the field began at 5 A.M. and lasted until 9 P.M. Its monotonous routine produced overpowering boredom. "When this war is over," a disgruntled Confederate swore, "I will whip the man that says 'fall in' to me."

Too often the officers were as uneducated as the men in their charge. "It is rather a funny operation for one man to teach another what he don't know himself," an Iowan commented. The colonel of the 5th Wisconsin was leading his first regimental drill when he lost his notes in the wind. In red-faced confusion he dismissed the men, who greeted the order with cat-calls.

Of course, officers eventually learned their duties and their troops learned routines. Yet the process took both time and patience.

Few diversions existed to break the tedium of army life. Letter-writing was a principal occupation; music, gambling, physical contests (such as baseball and wrestling), plus Bible-reading helped to pass some of the time.

An overindulgence in liquor created a number of problems, including profanity, fights, and insubordination. An Illinois private became convinced that "if there is any place on God's fair earth where wickedness 'stalketh abroad in daylight,' it is in the army."

Harsh environment, monotony of life, lack of recreational facilities, little contact with loved ones, reluctant adaptability to army life—all of these factors contributed to making Civil War soldiers chronic complainers.

Army rations received the loudest condemnations, as well they should, for human stomachs in the 1860s were subjected to some of the vilest concoctions ever devised by man and labeled as food.

The volunteer's independent nature led him easily to the traditional low opinion of superior officers. It was difficult to be obedient to one who had been a younger friend or neighbor back home, or who seemed unqualified for the position he held.

Soldiers' complaints extended to medical treatment, lack of good chaplains, insufficient uniforms, inadequate camp equipment, long marches, the weather, and army life in general. Johnny Rebs and Billy Yanks, unable to effect solutions, freely damned the problems. That too is part of army life.

The ultimate test of the Civil War soldier came in battle. Volunteers of North and South demonstrated throughout the conflict that while they might not be the best disciplined soldiers in America, they were among America's bravest fighters. For four bloody years they carried on their shoulders the heaviest responsibilities ever placed on this country's common folk, and they did it so valiantly that thirteen decades later we still marvel at their manliness, endurance, courage, and sacrifice.

Naturally, some acts of cowardice occurred in a war whose scope went far beyond every soldier's imagination. Overshadowing those weak incidents by a hundredfold were deeds of gallantry in every battle. Winston Churchill did not exaggerate when he wrote of Civil War soldiers: "Uncommon valor became common virtue."

Columns of men attacking amid a storm of gunfire would often lean forward as if they were advancing into a heavy rainstorm. Privates leaped forward to take command when officers fell. Men eagerly volunteered to become color-bearers, knowing full well that the man carrying the flag would be the primary target of enemy riflemen. The failure of one assault did not stop others being launched over the same ground. At the 1862 battle of Fredericksburg, the Union army attacked thirteen consecutive times in a futile effort to break the Confederate line.

Soldiers of blue and gray fought, and 700,000 of them died, in a war that remains the central theme of American history. From first to last, Johnny Rebs and Billy Yanks displayed heroism without indulging in heroics. Ray Carson has done a commendable job in portraying these common soldiers of the Civil War. It is impossible to capture the full depth of feeling experienced by the men of blue and gray, but the images herein give a clearer picture of army life and field service than is usually found in modern studies.

It is often said that an army is only as good as the general who leads it. However, at least two prominent Civil War figures believed the reverse to be true: a commander is only as good as the men he leads. Union general Joshua L. Chamberlain observed after the war: "The muster rolls on which the name and oath were written were pledges of honor—redeemable at the gates of death. And they who went up to them, knowing this, are on the lists of heroes."

In the middle of the Civil War, Confederate general Braxton Bragg made an even stronger statement: "We have had in great measure to trust to the individuality and self-reliance of the private soldier. Without the incentive or the motive which controls the officers . . . without hope of reward, he has, in this great contest, justly judged that the cause was his own, and gone into it with a determination to conquer or die. . . . History will yet award the main honor where it is due—to the private soldier."

James I. Robertson, Jr.
Virginia Tech

∽ Preface

As a pivotal point in our nation's history, the Civil War holds a special fascination in the hearts and minds of the American people. It was a war fought entirely by Americans, often dividing families and even pitting "brother against brother." But despite four years of bloodshed and deep ideological division, it created a united America stronger and more certain of its direction as a democratic nation.

Of course, the Civil War's impact is still felt in our society today. Many of the ideological and cultural differences continue to provoke impassioned opinions among our people. Its cost and effects changed the course of millions of lives and influenced the views of their descendants today. And no other war has been examined and written about more than this one.

Numerous Civil War history books discuss tactics, battles, and major figures. The three million individual soldiers who fought and sacrificed are relegated to anonymous numbers, unknown pawns in the grand scope of history. Yet it must be remembered that each of the numbers was a human being—men with hopes, dreams, and families who left it all behind to fight for their beliefs. Their fate affected all of their loved ones. More than 600,000 lost their lives, and an equal number of men were physically and/or mentally maimed for the rest of their lives. Many of the men never even actually saw battle, with over half of the deaths caused by disease—often within mere weeks of

enlisting. Despite this, most of them stayed and carried out their duties. Men from both sides of the conflict demonstrated courage and determination with a strong conviction that their cause was right. It is their story that I want this book to recount.

Ten years ago I began participating in Civil War reenacting, a hobby that appeals to thousands of Americans from all backgrounds. On any given weekend, reenactors gather at events throughout the country to immerse themselves in the past. Everything is done as it was 130 years ago, utilizing reproductions of the clothing, equipment, food, and shelter. All aspects of the soldiers' camp life are recreated with painstaking accuracy, including personal items such as toothbrushes made of ivory or combs made of wood. This attention to detail allows both reenactors and onlookers to personalize the past and experience a living history. For the reenactor there are special times when all the conditions are just right and a magical moment occurs. The present fades away, the veil of time draws back, and you suddenly feel as if you have actually stepped into the past.

As a photojournalist I've found this concept of time travel intriguing—a chance to capture a long-gone era on film in a realistic manner. Photography was in its infancy at the time of the Civil War, and the technical limitations, including extremely long exposures, make actual photographs of the time seem inert and outdated. Today's photographic equipment can literally capture the blink of an eye. It creates a sense of intimacy and intensity, allowing the viewer to experience the world through the eyes of the photographer. Visual images play an important role in how we perceive and deal with our world. By dressing as a reenactor and carrying my cameras in a haversack, I found a way to create images from an insider's point of view, thereby giving readers an opportunity to step back in time and enjoy a sense of "being there." It also allowed me to capture unposed moments in a more candid way. I then hand-colored these black-and-white images using a style similar to that of the 1860s.

Visual images alone cannot portray the entire story, however. I wanted my book to encourage the reader to better understand the Civil War soldier as a fellow individual. People identify with the past by way of the thoughts of folks like themselves, their similar emotions, hopes, and goals. By including first-person accounts from the diaries and letters of the soldiers, the war can be seen through their eyes. These writings personalize the trials and tribulations the men experienced, often more eloquently than any historian could.

Through these antiquated words and modern images of the common soldier, we can see ourselves and, at the same time, gain a better view of our past.

Ray M. Carson
Gainesville, Florida

CHAPTER ONE

A Rush to Glory—Joining Up

The seeds of the Civil War were sown within the very documents that founded our country. In the Declaration of Independence, Thomas Jefferson stated that all men were created equal and that there should be liberty and justice for all. Yet the Constitution itself contained contradictions that reflected the diverging paths of Northern and Southern culture. It allowed for slavery with the Fugitive Slave Act but levied a higher state tax and less congressional representation of Southern states with large slave populations. One could say that the Founding Fathers viewed slavery as a moral wrong but a constitutional right.

Also, to many people, the Union was a marriage between sovereign states, and any state had the right to divorce itself from the Union if it became untenable. This view was held not only by Southerners. Seven unsuccessful secession movements occurred between 1798 and 1856, five in the Northern states. Moreover, slavery died out in the North as much for economic reasons as moral ones: Slaves needed food, clothing, shelter, and medical care to keep them healthy enough to work. But the industrial North, with its large influx of immigrant labor, factories always had a fresh supply of workers willing to toil for low wages. Slavery probably would have died out in the South, as well, except for Eli Whitney's invention of the cotton gin, which greatly reduced the labor and cost of production, thereby increasing profits.

No special skills or training were necessary to pick cotton. This made slavery profitable and gave the Southern economy a highly sought after product— more than half of the export product for the United States by 1850. But "King Cotton" also caused more economic friction between the North and South. Since most manufacturing plants were in the North, Southerners had to ship the raw cotton north to refine it to cloth—and Northern manufacturers raised their production fees to increase profits. Plus the federal government passed higher tariffs on exports, so in the view of Southerners, both the federal government and Northern industry dictated the South's economy.

UNDER THE STARRY CROSS

A red rag, (there be those that say)—a red rag tied to a stick, and that is all! And yet—that red rag, crossed with blue, with white stars sprinkled the cross within, tied to a slim barked pine sapling, with leather thongs cut from a soldier's shoe, this rough red rag my soul loved with a lover's love.

SGT. BERRY BENSON
1ST SOUTH CAROLINA VOLUNTEERS

The two regions were also growing apart cultur-
ally, with the South's agriculturally based economy
developmentally static while the North's economy—
and population base—grew, thanks to technology and
industry. To Southerners, all these factors contributed
to the rapid erosion of their economy, culture, and
political power.

Further, a small but vocal minority of Northern
Abolitionists not only crusaded against slavery, they
also advocated that the federal government outlaw it.

As the North grew rapidly in population, settlers
moved west, creating new territories and states.
Debate over whether these states would be admitted
as free or slave brought America even closer to Civil
War.

The issue finally came to a head in 1854 with the
Kansas-Nebraska Act, which allowed the two new
states to decide for themselves whether to be free or
slave states. Kansas quickly became a battleground for
extremists from both sides. The situation quickly
turned violent, and the state became known as
"Bleeding Kansas." In 1859, one fanatical abolitionist
named John Brown, with a small group of followers,
seized the Federal armory at Harpers Ferry, Virginia,
hoping to create a slave insurrection. Captured, tried,
and executed for treason and murder, Brown became
a potent symbol for both sides—a martyr to the
Northern abolitionists and a dangerous extremist to
Southerners.

It was in this turbulent atmosphere that the election of 1860 was held. Within hours of Abraham Lincoln's election, the South Carolina legislature voted
unanimously to secede. Within weeks they were followed by six other states, and on February 8, 1861,
delegates from these states elected a Confederate government. Federal forts and armories were seized by
state militias and in Charleston, South Carolina, the
militia demanded the surrender of the federal garrison
at Fort Sumter. When the deadline passed on April
12, 1861, Fort Sumter was shelled. War was now
inevitable. The Confederacy was in open rebellion
and had committed an act of war by firing on a federal garrison.

OLD CONFEDERATE GENERAL

*I must go with the South, though the action is in the last
degree ungrateful. I owe all that I am to the government of
the United States. It had educated and clothed me with
honor. To leave the service is a hard necessity, but I must
go. Though I am resigning my position, I trust I may
never draw my sword against the old flag.*

GEN. JOSEPH E. JOHNSTON, C.S.A.

WINTER SERENADE

At midnight, a brass band which I think came on an
incoming train played some five or six pieces, the last of
which was "Home Sweet Home." As the familiar strains
of the grand old piece stole through the midnight air they
seemed to me like sweet echoes from the bending skies
which wake a thousand thoughts of other days, of home
and friends far away, that perhaps I will never see again;
of happy scenes in the peaceful days of childhood that now
return no more; all rushed in solemn troops through my
memory as sadly as a weird night wind that sighs and
moans through the strings of a broken harp.

PVT. GEORGE M. NEESE
CHEW'S BATTERY, VIRGINIA ARTILLERY

Neither side had any concept of the horrors of war that they would encounter over the next four years. John Billings, a Union army artilleryman, reflected on the naive misconceptions held by both sides:

The leading abolitionist had argued that the South was too cowardly to fight for slavery; and the South had been told by the fire-eaters . . . that the North could not be kicked into fighting. Alas! How little did either party understand the temper of the other!

Patriotic fervor now ran high on both sides. Towns organized recruitment drives and financed regiments. Women handmade flags and uniforms in both the North and South. Men responded to the call by the thousands. By July 1861 the Union army had swelled from a prewar strength of 13,000 to 186,000.

IRISH MELODY

One evening, a Confederate band came to the front and played "Dixie." Immediately across the way, a Union band responded with "John Brown's Body." The Confederates retaliated with "The Bonnie Blue Flag" and received "The Star Spangled Banner" in return. The music ceased; silence descended over the battle arena. Then a lone Union bugler played the notes of "Home Sweet Home." As the sweet sounds rose and fell on the evening air . . . all listened intently. I don't believe there was a dry eye in those assembled thousands.

PVT. LELANDER COGSWELL
11TH NEW HAMPSHIRE INFANTRY

Similar numbers boosted the ranks of the newly formed Confederate army.

But this was a generation that had only heard of war from fathers and grandfathers and whose concept of war came from novels and history books, replete with visions of heroic deeds and martial splendor. Many had never even traveled more than twenty miles from home. Joining the army offered them a chance to play soldier, see the country, and have a grand adventure. Everyone believed that the war would be over in a matter of weeks—a few quick battles, the enemy defeated, and they could all return to their homes as heroes. A young Confederate expressed the sentiment of many recruits: "I was a mere boy and carried away by boyish enthusiasm. I was tormented by feverish anxiety before I joined my regiment for fear the fighting would be over before I got into it."

These early volunteers were a cross section of American culture, and all brought a strong conviction that their cause was just. In the agricultural South, 69 percent of the enlistees were farmers, and 90 percent were native born. In the more industrial North, the enlistees were more evenly split between 48 percent farmers and 40 percent mechanics or laborers. The Northern cities also contained large immigrant populations, with hundreds of thousands of German, Irish, and English immigrant, fighting for their new homeland, making up one-fourth of the Union army.

The average age of both armies was twenty-five, yet numerous enlistees were much younger. Many just barely in their teens joined as drummer boys, considered noncombatants. Thousands of underage boys bluffed their way into both armies. A favorite trick was to slip a piece of paper in their shoe with the number *18* written on it. They could then truthfully swear that they were indeed "over 18." Older men also rushed to join. The 37th Iowa Infantry, nicknamed the Graybeards, had 145 soldiers sixty or older.

Illiteracy was common. One of every four Confederates could not read or write. The North had a better educational system, and their rates of uneducated were much lower. However, every Union regiment held illiterate soldiers.

Beyond a quest for adventure, the reasons for joining were greatly varied. For every Union soldier who joined to abolish slavery, dozens had little regard for or even outright hatred toward slaves. Some even blamed the slaves for causing the war, and many Union volunteers from the working class viewed the freedom of slaves as an economic threat for already scarce jobs. Some deemed Southern plantation owners despotic aristocrats whose feudal system threatened democracy. Most fought simply for preservation of the Union. From their Northern perspective, the Revolutionary War was fought to establish a united democratic country under one central government, and they viewed Southern secessionists as traitors intent on dissolving the country their forefathers had fought to create.

Southerners fought for the same motives but with an opposite viewpoint. To them the country was a union of individual states, each having the right to decide its own laws and economic structure. They considered the North an invader, attempting to conquer the people and politics of the South for its own economic gain. Southerners believed the federal government was attempting to destroy the Constitution by infringing on the rights of the individual.

The perpetuation of slavery was not a major issue to the average Southern soldier. Only one in ten Southerners owned slaves, and in an army mainly comprised of farmers, the ratio was even smaller. Although many Confederates viewed blacks as inferior, they had no fondness for the plantation owner, either. A Confederate soldier's opinion on slavery was often based on economic and cultural survival. With one-third of the southern population being slaves, the abolition of slavery would bring fierce competition for land and jobs, plus change the political structure. Some supported slavery simply because they felt the North had no right to dictate the policies of the South.

The strong beliefs held by each side divided the nation—and often families, as well. Mary Todd Lincoln, the president's wife, lost two brothers and a brother-in-law in the Confederate army. Union general Phillip St. George Cook had two sons in the Confederate army, and his daughter was married to Confederate general Jeb Stuart. Pennsylvania-born brothers William and Wesley Culp joined opposing armies: William enlisted in the 87th Pennsylvania and Wesley joined the 2nd Virginia. Wesley would see his family home one last time in the battle of Gettysburg on Culp's Hill—where he was killed.

Some men enlisted for the practical reason of a steady paycheck. Especially in the North, with its high unemployment rates, a soldier's pay of thirteen dollars a month drew many men to the army. As the war progressed and casualties mounted, joining up for patriotic ideals declined. To replace losses, both governments offered bounties of one hundred dollars or more to enlist. Although this brought a flood of volunteers, their incentive was different from the early volunteers. A man could only spend the bounty if he survived. As a result, these men tended to be less motivated in combat and diminished the morale and effectiveness of the units they served in.

The situation was made worse by the enactment of conscription laws to fill the depleted ranks. Not only did draftees make unwilling soldiers, but both sides allowed conscripts to buy a substitute to serve their enlistment. With fees starting at $300 only the rich could buy their way out. This caused great resentment among the civilian population and veteran troops. The cry of "rich man's war, poor man's fight" became a common complaint. On July 12, 1863, over 50,000 people rioted in New York City to protest the draft. Union troops finally subdued the mobs but not before some 1,000 civilians had been killed or wounded. Recruitment brokers supplied substitutes for a fee—often criminals or men totally unfit for duty. Bounty jumpers would enlist and desert numerous times under assumed names. One Massachusetts regiment received 186 bounty recruits of whom 115 deserted at the first opportunity. Veteran troops despised the bounty recruits. One Union officer referred to them as "the grandest scoundrels that ever went unhung." Veterans referred to them as "the scum of the slums." Ironically, this strengthened the resolve of the veterans to see the war to a conclusion. Reenlistments among veteran troops increased. Ben Falls of the 19th Massachusetts expressed the sentiment of many veterans when he stated, "If the new men won't finish the job, the old men must."

One group of men eagerly wanted to join the Union army, but they were refused until late 1862. Blacks saw the war as their chance at freedom and were willing and anxious to fight for it. The Union government was reluctant, knowing that popular sentiment would not support a war over slavery. Plus prejudice was a factor. Many viewed blacks as lazy and lacking the intelligence or courage to make good soldiers. When they finally were allowed into the Union army, desertion rates among white troops surged dramatically. But blacks compensated for the loss by providing over 185,000 men to serve the Union. They weren't treated equally as soldiers.

Initially they were given inferior equipment and assigned to strictly manual labor, and they were paid only half as much as white troops until 1864. But when they did get the opportunity, they proved that they could fight, and then attitudes toward them began to change. The 1st and 3rd Louisiana Colored Volunteers received high praise for their bravery at Port Hudson. The 54th Massachusetts proved the tenacity of black soldiers during their assault at Fort Wagner, suffering 272 casualties. By the end of the war, black Union troops had fought in thirty-three major engagements and had been awarded twenty-one Medals of Honor.

For all their perceived differences, the soldiers on both sides held a great deal in common. They were all Americans with the same language, culture, and history. They all shared similar hopes, dreams, and values with a powerful belief in God and family. And they all held dear the ideals of American democracy and the Constitution.

However, for the next four years these same Americans were willing to kill each other. Each side viewed the other as the enemy of that most sacred of American ideals: liberty.

THE 54TH

We called upon them in the day of our trial, when volunteering had ceased, when the draft was a partial failure, and the bounty system a senseless extravagance. They were ineligible for promotion, they were not to be treated as prisoners of war, nothing was definite except they could be shot and hanged as soldiers. Fortunate, indeed, it is for us, as well as for them, that there were equals to the crisis; that the grand historic moment which comes to a race only once in many centuries came to them, and they recognized it. They say that the day of their redemption had arrived.

COL. NORWOOD P. HALLOWELL
55TH MASSACHUSETTS INFANTRY

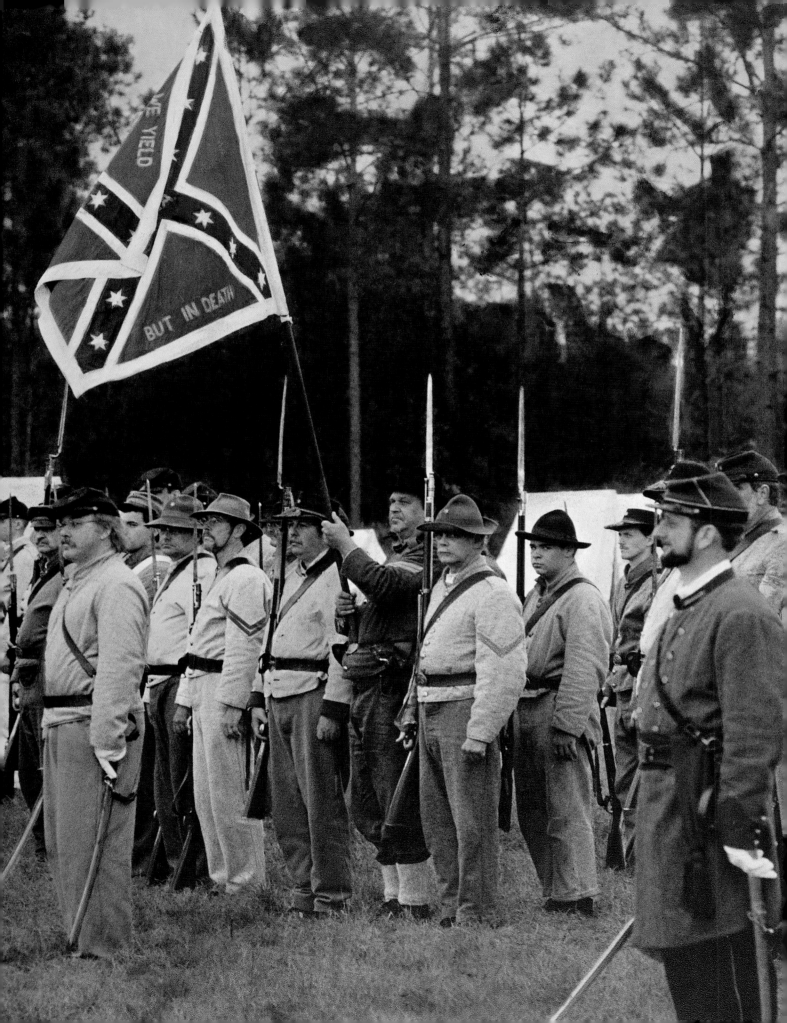

A UNION PRIVATE MADE $13 A MONTH AND HIS CONFEDERATE COUNTERPART $11. SINCE BOTH ARMIES PROVIDED FOOD, CLOTHING, AND SHELTER, A SOLDIER USED HIS PAY TO PURCHASE PERSONAL ITEMS SUCH AS ADDITIONAL FOOD OR ENTERTAINMENT. MANY MARRIED SOLDIERS SENT THE PAY TO THEIR FAMILIES. ALTHOUGH THEY WERE SUPPOSED TO BE MUSTERED FOR PAY EVERY OTHER MONTH, PAYDAY WAS OFTEN DELAYED—SOMETIMES BY AS MUCH AS SIX MONTHS.

YIELD BUT IN DEATH

The officers and men all being raw recruits, discipline was very galling to them, and as they would be brought under rigid military discipline a large amount of first class swearing could be heard every day. But soon the boys began to learn the "old soldier" tricks and learned to yield gracefully to the inevitable when they could not dodge the officers.

JAMES R. BINFORD
15TH MISSISSIPPI INFANTRY

CHAPTER TWO

Civilian to Soldier— Training and Equipment

Any ideas that the new recruits had about the army being a grand adventure were quickly dispelled on reaching training camp when they suddenly found their lives entirely controlled by military protocol. The enlistee was no longer an individual, just a small part in a giant machine called the army. He was told when to sleep, eat, and work as well as what to wear. His time was controlled by drum and bugle calls.

A recruit's first experience with army life was the issuance of uniforms and equipment. Government-issue clothing varied greatly in quality and fit. Poor workmanship and inferior cloth were common. Soldiers complained of receiving clothing several sizes too large or small, whose dye ran when it rained and seams split at the slightest strain. Leather shoes called "brogans" were often universal with no left or right. Stiff and ill fitting, they were called "pontoons" by the soldiers, and one even joked that they were big enough to double as a writing desk.

Many of the early regiments brought their own uniforms, supplied by patriotic citizens or state armories. These uniforms were often colorful and outrageously fancy. A popular style on both sides was modeled after the French army's elite Zouaves. Others reflected the ethnic background of the unit. The 79th New York, known as the Highlanders, went to war in kilts and tartan plaid pants.

Although symbols of unit pride, these fancy uniforms were ill suited for field duty, and most troops opted for the plainer but more comfortable army-issue uniform. The variety of uniforms could also have tragic consequences in battle. The 7th New York went to war in gray uniforms, and several Confederate regiments wore dark blue. In the fear and confusion of early battles, regiments occasionally fired on their own armies. In the North, the standard uniform became a dark-blue hip-length wool jacket, sky-blue wool trousers, and muslin shirt and drawers. The jacket was referred to as a sack coat, and soldiers joked that, indeed, it had all the comfort and fit of a burlap sack.

RAMMING THE CHARGE

At Gettysburg, when the artillery fire was at its height, a brawny fellow, who seemed happy at the prospect for a hot time, broke out singing:
   "Backward, roll backward, O Time in thy flight;
    Make me a child again, just for this fight!"
Another fellow near him replied, "Yes, and a gal child at that."

PVT. CARLTON MCCARTHY
2ND COMPANY, RICHMOND HOWITZERS

In the Confederacy, due to the shortages of fabric and dyes, the uniform became more varied as the war continued. Southern soldiers often relied on clothes sent from families back home, and their uniforms were a kaleidoscope of grays and browns. After gray, the most common color was a yellowish brown, called butternut, dyed with walnut shells.

Headgear was a matter of personal choice, although some units, such as the Iron Brigade, adopted distinctive hats as a symbol of unit pride. The forage cap was standard issue in both armies, but many men opted for a more useful wide-brimmed felt hat referred to as a slouch hat. Its brim provided protection against sun and rain and could be tied down with a scarf to act as earmuffs in cold weather.

Soldiers were supposed to receive two coats, three pairs of trousers, and four pairs of shoes each year. But both armies, especially the Confederacy, had trouble maintaining this quota. Soldiers became adept at mending and carried small sewing kits called "housewives." They often wore the same clothes for months on end, repairing them until they fell apart or could be replaced. The poor condition of their clothing caused one Confederate to quip, "One hole in the seat of the breeches indicates a captain, two holes a lieutenant, and the seat of the pants all wore out indicates that the individual is a private."

A recruit's equipment all added up to a burdensome weight. In addition to clothing, he initially received a blanket, poncho, leather cartridge box and belt, cloth haversack for food, canteen, weapon, bayonet and scabbard, backpack, heavy great coat, and "shelter halve." Combined with personal items, the total load could easily exceed fifty pounds. One recruit complained in a letter home that he felt more like a packhorse than a soldier. Most veterans learned to dispense with everything except the essentials and went for comfort.

The second surprise to the new enlistee was the regimentation of army life. To create an effective force, drills and discipline had to be practiced until they became automatic. Obedience to orders had to be instinctive. Solders were awakened by drum call at five o'clock in the morning; they had fifteen minutes

VOLLEY FIRE

On came the yelling horde until within—it seemed to us—not over twenty-five yards. It was an anxious and critical moment, and it afforded Colonel Pickett an opportunity to see of what stuff his regiment was made. Suddenly came the order "Twenty-Fifth ready"; and like clockwork every rifle was in position; "Aim," and every eye was glancing along the rifle barrel; "Fire!" and that volley, almost like a single shot, sent death and dismay into the Rebel host.

PVT. SAMUEL PUTNAM
25TH MASSACHUSETTS VOLUNTEERS

to dress and fall in for roll call. Breakfast and infirmary call then lasted until eight o'clock, when guard mount was posted. The rest of the troops drilled until noon, a break for lunch, and more drilling until 4:30 in the afternoon. They were then released to clean up for formal inspection and official orders at 5:45. Afterward the soldiers were dismissed for dinner until 8:30, when final roll call sounded. At nine o'clock taps played, and all lights were extinguished. The only variation to this routine was the addition of church service and a regimental inspection on Sunday.

The recruits found this schedule tedious and complained that they had joined to fight, not drill. Oliver Norton of the 83rd Pennsylvania summed up the feeling of many soldiers: "The first thing in the morning

THE MANY HOURS OF DRILL THE RECRUITS FACED COVERED
ALL ASPECTS OF BECOMING A TRAINED SOLDIER INCLUDING
THE USE OF THE BAYONET IN HAND-TO-HAND COMBAT. BUT
THE IMPROVED RANGE AND KILLING POWER OF THE RIFLED
MUSKET WAS CHANGING THE STYLE OF WARFARE. HAND-TO-
HAND COMBAT BECAME LESS FREQUENT. ONLY ONE PERCENT
OF THE INJURIES IN THE CIVIL WAR WERE INFLICTED BY
BAYONET.

is drill, then drill, then drill again. Then drill, drill, a
little more drill. Then drill and lastly drill. Between
drills we drill, and sometimes we stop to eat a little
and have roll call." For these civilians turned soldiers,
military maneuvers were an entirely foreign concept.
Many didn't know left from right, and sergeants
sometimes tied hay to the left foot and straw to the
right foot of a new recruit, then marched them, yelling,
"Hayfoot! Strawfoot!" until they got the concept.
Most of the officers were as raw as the recruits. In
the beginning of the war, officers were elected by the
troops or were political appointees from the state governments, so they had no more experience than the
men they were supposed to train. Drill practice was
often literally "by the book," with officers reading

THE COMING STORM

"There come orders" were the words that passed from lip to lip. Without commands the lines are formed; the cannoneers stood by their guns; the drivers stood with hand on rein and foot in stirrup, ready to mount. The eye lighted up, the arm again grew strong, and the nerves were again growing steady.

CAPT. JAMES R.CARNAHAN
86TH INDIANA VOLUNTEERS

from the manuals as troops attempted the maneuvers. Through sheer repetition, the soldiers and officers became drill proficient. Additionally, both armies adapted policies of appointing officers by a review board, based on their leadership and performance abilities rather than popularity. This improved the quality and leadership command of the officers.

Recruits also had to be trained in target practice. Both armies had trouble supplying weapons for the suddenly vast armies, and troops received a variety of muskets. Many of the early supplies were heavy .69- and .75-caliber smoothbores from European arsenals. The soldiers called them "pumpkin slingers" and found them terribly inaccurate. At one practice only 3 of the 160 rounds hit a barrel at 180 yards. Union general Ulysses S. Grant complained that "a man could fire at you all day without you even finding out." Some of these smoothbores used "buck and ball" ammunition. Comprised of one full-sized ball and three smaller ones, it created a modified shotgun and improved the odds of hitting something. Quarter-masters in both armies tried to standardize the weapons, and the .58-caliber Springfield and Enfield muskets became the preferred weapons, although they comprised only 40 percent of the arsenals. With a rifled barrel, the Springfield could pierce six inches of pine board at 500 yards and was a great improvement in firepower. But it took eleven motions to load the weapon and at best a soldier could fire three rounds in one minute.

An effectively run army required organization and record keeping. Food, clothing, and equipment had to be purchased, transported, and maintained. Supporting every combat regiment was an equal number of clerks, quartermasters, teamsters, wagoneers, blacksmiths, and other noncombatants.

GUARDING THE PORT

Spent the day in the usual way. Two hours of gun drill in the morning, then a game of ball, and hour of company drill in the afternoon, a game or two of chess, then parade at 4:00 PM. Reading, writing the remainder of the time till retreat at 8:00 PM when I made down my cot. In the quiet of alone, I lay down, a few yearning thoughts of home, mother, etc. and all is oblivion till reveille calls me forth from the land of nod.

PVT. JENKIN JONES
6TH WISCONSIN INFANTRY

NEW RECRUITS HAD TO BE TAUGHT TO CLEAN AND CARE FOR THEIR WEAPONS. RUST AND POWDER FOULING COULD QUICKLY MAKE A RIFLE USELESS, AND WEAPON INSPECTION BECAME A DAILY ROUTINE FOR THE NEW SOLDIER.

A LITTLE MENDING

Here is a comrade writing a letter home; another reading a paper, smoking the while; another is doing a bit of mending; and others are having a game. Old Sledge may be with the same old greasy cards that have done duty for so many months. Old comrade, tell me, is this not real comfort?

PVT. SAMUEL PUTNAM
COMPANY A, 25TH MASSACHUSETTS VOLUNTEERS

Despite their training, most soldiers never became good marksmen. It is estimated that for every man hit, 900 pounds of lead were expended. To make their firepower more effective, officers generally relied on volleys fired by companies or regiments. This sent hundreds of bullets hurtling toward the enemy at chest-high level, increasing the odds of a hit. Effective volley fire could decimate a line in a matter of seconds.

Infantry was the backbone of both armies, providing 80 percent of the combat troops. Soldiers were organized by companies of seventy to one hundred men. Ten companies combined to form a regiment, and four regiments made up a brigade.

Although regiments were supposed to contain 1,000 men, most usually had about 600 due to disease and desertion. Many quickly became even smaller after combat losses. The 22nd Massachusetts went to war with 1,177 men but within a year was worn down to 200.

Men had great pride and loyalty in their regiments and flags and often considered all other units to be inferior outsiders. They had even less love for the other branches of service and derided them whenever possible. To maintain unit pride, both armies tended to create new regiments rather than replace losses. The disadvantage of this policy was that veteran units were bled dry and disbanded, while new regiments were sent into combat with little experience.

DURING CAMPAIGNS AGAINST THE NAVAJO INDIANS IN THE 1850S, AN ARMY SURGEON NAMED A. J. MEYER EXPERIMENTED WITH WAYS OF IMPROVING COMMUNICATIONS OVER LONG DISTANCES. USING A SYSTEM OF FLAGS BY DAY AND TORCHES BY NIGHT, HE WAS ABLE TO TRANSMIT MESSAGES BETWEEN UNITS. IN THE CIVIL WAR, BOTH ARMIES CREATED SIGNAL CORPS TO IMPROVE COMMUNICATIONS. BESIDES RELAYING COMMANDS FROM HEADQUARTERS, SIGNALMEN WERE PLACED ON ANY HIGH GROUND IN A BATTLE TO TRANSMIT MESSAGES BETWEEN REGIMENTS.

Although the infantry made up the majority of the troops, military organization required large numbers of support troops. Many men never saw combat, being assigned as clerks, orderlies, blacksmiths, bakers, and wagoneers.

The Quartermaster Corps supplied all the needs of the army, including shelter, equipment, transportation, and clothing. Vast wagon trains followed the armies with an average of twenty-five wagons per 1,000 men. The Subsistence Department of the Commissary General supplied the food. Dry or packaged food was transported by wagon, but meat was sometimes "on the hoof," with herds of cattle following the armies. The Engineer Corps built fortifications, bridges, and roads for the armies. A new organization, the Signal Corps, transmitted commands by flag or telegraph to distant regiments.

Due to its industrial background, the Union artillery was superior throughout the war and outnumbered the Confederate guns two to one. Despite the soldiers' jokes about artillery always being in the rear, infantry troops came to respect and welcome any artillery support they could get.

The men who joined artillery tended to be better educated than the average solder since it took some knowledge of mechanics and mathematics to operate the guns. It also took a special type of bravery. Because artillery was usually located on high open ground for effective fire, it became a prime target for the enemy. Unlike infantrymen, artillerymen could not move from a fixed position and often had to perform under concentrated enemy fire. They also drilled more than other branches since a gun crew had to work as a team. Each man had a specific duty to perform. A well-trained crew of six could fire two rounds per minute, yet the loss of two or three positions could render a cannon useless. Artillery was organized by battery. A six-gun battery consisted of 156 men and 72 horses; 70 men operated the guns, and 52 of them took care of the horses and caissons. In battle, artillery's role was to provide concentrated firepower for as much devastation as possible. Veteran soldiers feared artillery more than any other type of fire because they could not fight back or hide from its destructive force. Much of the artillery's ordnance consisted of exploding shells filled with shrapnel or lead rifle balls. When they exploded, hot metal flew in all directions, causing numerous casualties. Once they got within 150 yards, men faced canister shot, turning cannons into giant shotguns, tearing huge gaps in the lines.

Cavalry was considered the elite service and drew many recruits from the wealthier classes. It conveyed a certain romanticism, with visions of fancy uniforms, riding noble steeds with flashing sabers, and charging into the fray. The reality was far different. With the increased range of weapons, cavalry charges were ineffective against massed infantry, and sabers were only useful in hand-to-hand combat. Indeed, many cavalrymen discarded their sabers in favor of pistols. Cavalry's effectiveness was based on its mobility. It became the eyes of the army as scouts, and was used for sudden hit-and-run actions, disrupting enemy supply lines.

The cavalry was generally despised by the infantry. Since they weren't used in front-line fighting, infantrymen rarely saw them in action. A common jibe from the infantry was "Ever see a dead cavalryman?" Yet despite the opinion of the rest of the army, the cavalry served an important purpose and could be a deciding factor in the outcome of a battle.

END OF A LONG DAY

I remember two things in particular after I got home for good. It was hard for me to sit in a chair or sleep in a bed. In the army, only captains and up had chairs. I hadn't sat in a chair for three years or about that. As for beds, they were too soft to sleep in. For a long time, I preferred to sleep and to sit on the floor.

PVT. ROBERT H. STRONG
UNION ARMY

CHAPTER THREE

Far from Home—Camp Life

The army could train soldiers in drilling and marksmanship, but it couldn't prepare them for the rigors and monotony of outdoor camp life. Early camps were a disaster. Although the regular army had rules for proper camp layout and sanitation, most of the volunteer regiments were entirely composed of civilian recruits who had little understanding of military rules—and even less of the relationship between sanitation and disease. Camps were laid out in a completely haphazard manner. Soldiers pitched tents on low ground that turned into a quagmire with every rain. In dry times, dust kicked up by thousands of feet covered everything, including food. Human and animal waste littered the camps, and food and water supplies quickly became polluted by misplaced and overused latrines and bathing facilities.

Through trial and error, the troops found ways to improve their living conditions. They discovered that spreading straw or pine boughs on the ground kept it dry and soft. They learned to separate the camp from the latrines and water supplies. Veterans knew not to touch the sides of their tent in a rainstorm or it would leak. They also learned to work together with their tentmates to ease the daily workload. Sgt. Rice Bull of the 123rd New York described the delegation of duties at the start of every day: "Each group of men who formed a mess began their labors; one took canteens and went for water, another acted as cook and prepared breakfast; the remaining man pulled down the tent and packed up."

Since a soldier spent weeks or even months between battles, shelter was a primary concern. Early in the war, larger tents such as the conical Shipley were used. Designed for ten people, they often contained as many as twenty. In such cramped quarters, the men would sleep by spooning: Laying in a circle with feet toward the center pole, they would all face the same direction. If a soldier wanted to turn over, he had to wake the others, and they would all roll over on command. But these tents proved too cumbersome on campaign, and most soldiers resorted to the A-frame or dog tent. Two soldiers would combine their six-foot-by-four-foot shelter halves to create a satisfactory tent. They then combined their blankets and ponchos, one of each on the bottom and top, and slept together between them.

TWILIGHT CAMP

We were awaken at an early mornings hour . . . the rising sun sent its rays of light down like golden needles through the tops of the pine trees. Little fires were kindled, our coffee was quickly boiled, and we sat down to our rude breakfasts with appetites such as are unknown in lives of luxury and ease.

PVT. THEODORE GERRISH
UNION ARMY

In the Confederate army, with canvas in short supply, tents were rarely seen after 1863. Most Confederate soldiers either slept under a single blanket, or they built lean-tos or she-bangs from available wood and combined their blankets with a comrade's. In the more permanent winter camps, soldiers of both sides built log huts complete with an interior fireplace. A barrel with both ends knocked out served as a chimney.

Food was another primary concern. A soldier's main diet consisted of salt pork or beef, bread, cornmeal or hardtack crackers, potatoes, beans, and coffee. On the march, the fare was simplified to hardtack, salt pork, coffee, and sugar. In the Union army, the most plentiful and most scorned item was hardtack. A plain flour cracker three inches square and a half-inch thick, it was issued more for its durability than taste or nutritional value. Often too hard to bite into, it was soaked in coffee or grease or broken up with blows from a rifle butt or stone. Soldiers referred to them as "teeth dullers" or "sheet-iron crackers." For the Confederates, cornmeal was more frequent than hardtack, yet due to poor quality and supply, this was sometimes more husk and cob than actual meal. It was often mixed with pork grease to make a stew called "coosh" or formed as a bread, wrapped around a ramrod and baked over a fire. Another unpopular meal was a dried vegetable cube used in stew called "desiccated vegetables." The soldiers renamed it "desecrated" or "baled hay" and claimed it was absolutely tasteless.

The overall quality of the food varied greatly. Food was supplied to both armies by civilian contractors, and corruption was common. Because government contracts were usually awarded to lowest bidder, the quality of the soldiers' rations was abysmally poor. Beef was often rancid, with more fat than meat, and the bread and hardtack was often infested with weevils and worms. William Fletcher of the 1st Texas described one shipment of beef: "It was not necessary to have a peg to hang it on—throw it against a tree and it would stick. Need not necessarily be a nearby tree, as there was little danger if it being stolen." The meat was often so heavily salted or pickled that it had to be soaked in water before cooking.

ON CAMPAIGN, A SOLDIER WAS AT THE MERCY OF THE ELEMENTS AND OFTEN HAD LITTLE PROTECTION FROM RAIN OR COLD. OFTEN, HOLDING HIS CLOTHES AND BEDDING OVER A MEAGER FIRE WAS THE ONLY WAY TO DRY THEM OUT.

MORNING FROST

Night at last came on, and with it, rain, sleet, and snow. It also became much colder. Our overcoats being wet, froze stiff upon us, so 'twas with difficulty we could bend our bodies, and we had to stamp our feet, rub our hands, and dance about to keep them from freezing. Besides, the "Rebs" were becoming extremely annoying; they were popping away at us all the time, and we did not know what moment they would come out and pounce upon us, so we did not take off our boxes or leave our arms the entire night.

SGT. IRA BLANCHARD
COMPANY H, 20TH ILLINOIS

MORNING COFFEE

March 4th. We are up at day break, I am feeling none the worse from sleeping in my wet clothes, get a fire going and soon have a tin cup of steaming hot coffee, minus the sugar or milk, but it tastes like nectar just the same.

PVT. BENJAMIN T. SMITH
51ST ILLINOIS INFANTRY

Still, bad food was better than no food at all. Supplying food to vast armies in the field was a daunting task, and the quartermaster supply lines were often taxed beyond their limit. Troops on both sides suffered periods of starvation. Col. Robert Brown of the 64th Ohio recalled, "I have seen soldiers gather from horse's feet grains of corn which they had spilled while feeding, wash, dry, and grind in a coffee mill, and make it into mush."

For the Confederate soldier, the Union blockade made the situation worse. By 1863 many were surviving on one meal a day, and by 1865 some had only a handful of parched corn or the contents of the haversacks of the dead to satisfy their hunger.

In camp, boredom and loneliness were a soldier's worst enemies, and he kept as busy as possible to occupy his mind and soften the blow of separation from loved ones. Pvt. Henry Schafer of the 103rd Illinois stated that "almost everyone thought more about the best way to kill time than anything else." Among the literate, letter writing and reading were the most popular pastimes. Any reading material was considered a treasure to relieve the hours of boredom, especially during long winter encampments. Newspapers and books were passed around the company for every man to read. When opposing armies were settled close by, individual soldiers would sometimes call informal truces to trade newspapers between the lines.

Letter writing provided the soldiers with an emotional anchor to loved ones and normal home life amid the insanities of war. Any mail call created excitement and joy among the troops. Robert Goodyear of the 27th Connecticut wrote to his family, "The soldier looks upon a letter from home as a perfect God send—sent, as it were, by some kind, ministering Angel Spirit, to cheer his dark and weary hours."

Music was prevalent throughout a soldier's day. Drummers, fifers, and regimental bands were used to relay orders and regulate soldiers' activities. In addition, every regiment had individuals who would sing or play guitar, banjo, or fiddle for the entertainment of his fellow soldiers. More songs were written during

SOLDIERS LEARNED TO MAKE USE OF ANY FORM OF SHELTER THEY COULD DEVISE. ON CAMPAIGN, LOG STRUCTURES TOOK TOO MUCH ENERGY AND TIME TO CONSTRUCT, SO TENTS WERE OFTEN PITCHED ON ALREADY MUDDY OR FROZEN GROUND. TO AFFORD SOME COMFORT, SOLDIERS WOULD OFTEN EXCAVATE A LARGE PIT, BUILD WALLS OF DIRT OR HAY, AND USE SHELTER HALVES OR TREE BRANCHES FOR A ROOF. REFERRED TO AS A "SHE-BANG," THIS IMPROVISED SHELTER KEPT OUT WIND AND RAIN.

LETTER HOME

In the past three days, I have received a large mail which has excited the envy of my companions. Welcomed and with what eagerness the contents are read. Oh my friends, if correspondence ever was valued it is now. If you knew with what pleasure all the soldiers receive their letters or papers, I don't think there would be any slowness about writing often and long and on any subject.

PVT. EDWARD SCHILLING
COMPANY F, 4TH MARYLAND

As a substitute for bread on campaign, the Union army supplied its troops with a hard cracker made of plain flour called hardtack. Distributed more for its durability than taste, it was often rock hard and either moldy or bug-infested.

Most soldiers preferred to do their own cooking or combine supplies with several other soldiers to form a mess. Attempts to have company cooks usually failed since men assigned as cooks were unfit or unwilling for other duties and showed little or no effort.

THE ARMY SUPPLIED SOLDIERS WITH THE BARE ESSENTIALS NEEDED FOR MILITARY DUTY. OTHER ITEMS SUCH AS PAPER, PENCILS, GROOMING SUPPLIES, AND A VARIETY OF FOOD ITEMS WERE SUPPLIED BY INDEPENDENT MERCHANTS, KNOWN AS SUTLERS, WHO FOLLOWED THE ARMIES. FOLLOWING THE LAW OF SUPPLY AND DEMAND, THESE SUTLERS OFTEN CHARGED OUTRAGEOUS PRICES FOR THEIR WARES.

DESPITE THE HIGH PRICES, SOLDIERS BEGRUDGINGLY SPENT MUCH OF THEIR PAYCHECKS AT THE SUTLER'S TENT. FACED WITH A STEADY DIET OF HARDTACK AND SALT PORK, ANY VARIETY OF FOOD, SUCH AS A CAN OF PEACHES, WAS A GOURMET TREAT FOR THE SOLDIERS.

ROUNDERS

Camplife to a young man who has nothing specially to tie him to home has many attractions—abundance of company, continual excitement, and all the fun and frolic that a thousand lighthearted boys can devise. . . . Stories, cards, wrestling, boxing, racing, all these and a thousand other things enter into a day in camp. The roving, uncertain life of a soldier has a tendency to harden and demoralize most men. The restraints of home, family and society are not felt. The fact that a few hours may put them in battle, where their lives are not worth a fig, are forgotten.

LT. COL. JOHN BEATTY
3RD OHIO VOLUNTEERS

the Civil War than any other war. Although many were patriotic songs to stir the martial spirit, the most popular among the troops were the sentimental ballads such as "Home, Sweet Home" and "Lorena" that reminded them of loved ones and of home.

Games and sporting contests were popular with the younger troops. When boredom in camp overtook them, amusements such as rounders (baseball), checkers, foot races, or boxing matches would be quickly organized between companies or individuals. During the winter, companies and regiments would face off in snowball fights staged as mock battles.

Despite adverse conditions, the soldiers maintained their sense of humor. Tall tales and jokes made up much of the conversation around the campfire, and practical jokes were also common—often at the expense of visiting civilians or a neighboring company. In winter, pranksters would throw a wet blanket over someone's makeshift chimney, providing amusement for all onlookers as the coughing, gagging soldiers piled out of their smoke-filled shelter.

The men also enjoyed less wholesome activities. Gambling, especially dice and cards, was prevalent. A poker game could be found in any camp at any time. Soldiers would wager on almost any contest, including horse races, boxing matches, cockfights, and even flea races.

Alcohol, when available, was consumed with a passion. For the average soldier, liquor was prohibited and often hard to come by. But officers could purchase it from the commissary whenever they wanted, and subordinates wrote contemptuously about drunken officers.

When encamped near cities, some troops would slip away to brothels for a night of what they termed "horizontal refreshment." Despite the high moralistic tone of the era, prostitution was rampant near the camps. Washington claimed 450 registered brothels during the war; 82 of every 1,000 soldiers contracted venereal diseases. The only treatment was salts of mercury, and soldiers often jested: "A night with Venus, a lifetime with Mercury."

DISCIPLINE IN THE ARMY WAS A HARSH NECESSITY. TO CONTROL DRUNKENNESS, THEFT, GAMBLING, AND INSUBORDINATION, THE SOLDIER'S PUNISHMENT WAS OFTEN PHYSICAL LABOR OR HUMILIATION BEFORE HIS PEERS.

Not all of the men explored their vices. Many held deep religious beliefs and were shocked by what they saw in camp. Henry Schafer of the 103rd Illinois wrote to his wife:

In our camp wickedness prevails to almost unlimited extent. It looks to me as though some men try to see how depraved they can be. Gambling, card playing, profanity, Sabbath breaking, and c. are among the many vices practiced by many of the men. . . . It sometimes seems to me that the Almighty would never bless the efforts of our army to put down this rebellion while it is so depraved.

Many soldiers agreed with this sentiment, and the most popular book in camp was the Bible. Many men found a renewed interest in religion after being exposed to the hardships and death that surrounded their existence. Every regiment had a chaplain to provide religious service, spiritual comfort, and guidance.

The Civil War soldier was typical of his American background. Fiercely independent—and confident in his ability to run his own life—he did not take well to officers' orders or military regulations. Since companies were usually recruited from a single town, the soldiers saw little reason to take orders from someone who had been his equal at home. The boredom and vices of camp life only compounded the problem. To maintain discipline, military justice was often severe and humiliating. In addition to jail time or hard labor, a soldier could be sentenced to wearing a ball and chain, carrying a hefty log or a cannonball, or being "bucked and gagged"—his wrist and ankles tied together and a heavy stick inserted between bent knees and elbows for hours on end. Thieves had their heads shaved and were drummed out of camp. Captured deserters were executed by firing squad in front of the assembled regiments. Such harsh punishments had the desired effect by transforming these independent and often unruly soldiers into a disciplined, operational army. One officer gave the Civil War soldier high praise in an off-handed way: "They were the worst soldiers and the best fighting men I ever saw."

GETTING THE NEWS

Daily the newsboys make their appearance calling out, "Washington Chronicle and New York papers!" They enjoy an extensive patronage. With these sheets many moments are pleasantly spent, as their columns are eagerly perused.

WILLARD GLAZIER
FEDERAL CAVALRYMAN

HUNTING GRAYBACKS

The "salamander grayback" had more lives than a cat, and propagated its species more rapidly than a roe-herring. Once lodged in the seams of the clothing, there they remained till time mouldered the garments. You might scald, scour, scrub,clean, rub, purify or bury the rainment under ground, and you only had your trouble for the pains; they seemed to enjoy it and multiply under the process . . . Every evening in Maryland, when the army had halted and bivouacked for the night, hundreds of soldiers might be seen sitting half denuded on the road-side or in the fields, busily engaged in a relentless slaughter of the vermin.

PVT. ALEXANDER HUNTER
COMPANY A, 17TH VIRGINIA INFANTRY

PRAYER BEFORE BATTLE

Rose early, and it was supposed that a crossing would be made right away. Colonel Merrill called on the chaplain to offer a prayer. This performance didn't aid us a mite; it only unfitted us, if anything, for it reminded us of the danger of being wiped out before night.

PVT. JOHN W. HALEY
17TH MAINE REGIMENT

CHAPTER FOUR

Trials of the Flesh—Medicine, Surgery, and Doctoring

For the Civil War soldier, the greatest danger came not from battle but from disease. Many regiments were decimated, losing as much as 50 percent of their manpower before they ever saw combat. The 12th Connecticut went to war with 1,000 men yet had only 640 present at their first battle. Although the 22nd Massachusetts had 915 men on its roster, 588 of them were listed as "absent sick" in the autumn of 1862. Of the 394,557 men who gave up their lives for the Union, 227,580 died of disease. The Confederates fared no better, with 164,000 out of a total of 289,000 deaths due to disease.

Much of the problem came simply from the massive number of men who were suddenly thrust into makeshift army camps. Before the war, the United States Army consisted of fewer than 13,000 troops, yet by July 1861, more than 186,000 men had answered the call for volunteers. The newly formed Confederacy enjoyed similar conscription success. The U. S. Army's prewar medical staff consisted of thirty surgeons and eighty-three assistant surgeons. From this meager number, twenty-four resigned to join the Confederacy. Both sides suddenly had vast armies with overwhelmed and overworked medical staff and facilities. Even later in the war, the average ratio was one surgeon per 133 men in the Union army and one per every 324 men in the Confederate army.

Overcrowded camps with poor sanitation, combined with the rigors of outdoor living and poor diet, quickly turned into breeding grounds for infectious diseases that ravaged the troops. Morning reveille often was accompanied by the sounds of coughing, wheezing, and moaning as sick men rose to face another day.

WRITING HOME

My Dear Susan,
I received your letter of the 23rd of June on the 28th at night, after I had laid me down on my blanket to try and while away the lonely hours of the night. I cannot sleep at night but a little. . . . I imagine in those lonely night watches you too are awake lonely and sad. I strive then to turn my thoughts beyond the confines of earth and in all sincerity of heart try to lift my prayers to our Heavenly Father to spare us to meet again. And oh how earnestly I pray that death may not intervene to prevent our meeting—with my darling children around our own hearth stone.

MAJ. PATRICK A. MCGRIFF
12TH GEORGIA INFANTRY

LAST MAN DOWN

The worst condition to endure is when you fall wounded upon the field. Now you are helpless. No longer are you filled with the enthusiasm of battle. You are helpless—the bullets still fly over and about you—you are no longer able to shift your position or seek shelter. Every bullet that strikes near you is a new terror. Perchance you are able to take out your handkerchief, which you raise in supplication to the enemy not to fire in your direction and to your friends of your helplessness. This is a trying moment. How slowly time flies!

CAPT. FRANK HOLSINGER
19TH U.S. COLORED INFANTRY

Surgeon George Stevens of the 77th New York vividly described the effects that bad living conditions and disease had on his regiment.

Everything combined to exhaust the energies of the men to produce fevers, diarrhea, and scurvy. Day after day, the men toiled under a burning sun; night after night they were called to arms. Their clothing and tents were drenched in frequent rains, and they often slept in beds of mud. With the hot weather, malaria became more and more deadly. The hospitals became daily more crowded. The strongest are constantly falling. Men who worked at the breastworks one day would be found in the hospital on the next, burning with fever, tormented with insatiable thirst, racked with pains, or wild with delirium, their parched lips and teeth blackened with sores, the hot breath and sunken eyes, the sallow skin and trembling pulse, all telling of the violent workings of these diseases.

The leading killers were dysentery and typhoid fever. Together these diseases caused 73,894 deaths in the Union army that could have been avoided through proper sanitation and food preparation. In the first year of the war, 640 of every 1,000 Union soldiers suffered from dysentery. Chauncy Cooke of the 25th Wisconsin wrote to his mother, "The health of the regiment is none too good. One man dies on an average day. As I write this letter the drum is beating. The food we get is to blame for our bad health. The boys threaten to riot for the bad beef and spoilt bread that is issued to us." Cooke was right about the food. Bread and beef were the main staples of a soldier's diet, providing starch and proteins but seriously lacking in vitamins and roughage. Fresh vegetables and fruit were rare, and numerous cases of scurvy ravaged both armies.

To add to this misery, most troops came from rural areas with sparse populations, so many of the men had never been exposed to such childhood diseases as chicken pox, measles, mumps, or whooping cough.

With thousands of men suddenly crowded together, these diseases ran rampant. Measles alone killed 10,000 in both armies. Surgeon Legrand Wilson of the 42nd Mississippi described a visit to a makeshift hospital in a tobacco warehouse: "About one hundred sick men crowded in a room sixty by one hundred feet in all stages of measles. The poor boys lying on a hard floor, with only one or two blankets under them, not even straw, and anything they could find for a pillow. Many sick and vomiting, many already showing unmistakable signs of blood poisoning."

For many former city dwellers, living outdoors was especially difficult. Exposed to the elements, with

THE ASSISTANT SURGEON WAS RESPONSIBLE FOR THE UPKEEP OF THE SURGEON'S MEDICAL AREA. HE ALSO RECORDED THE SOLDIERS' INJURIES AND CONDITIONS AND MAINTAINED MEDICAL SUPPLIES.

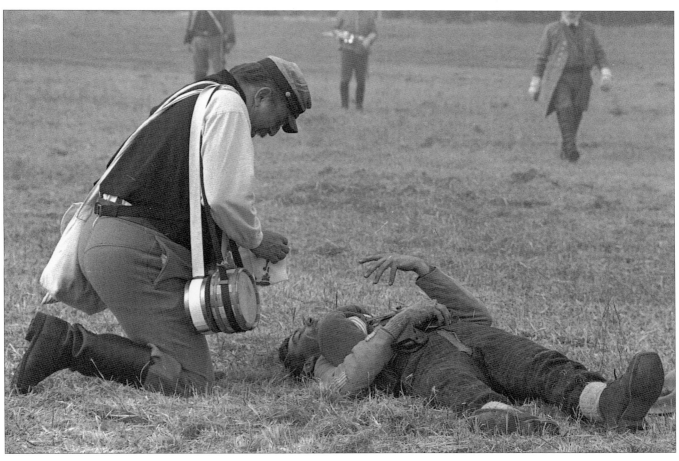

HELPING HAND

We sprang forward, but before we reached the head of the regiment, I was struck with a minnie ball which passed completely through the right shoulder completely shattering and rendering that important member helpless. It did not bring me to the ground as is generally the case when one is hit with a minnie ball, nor cause much pain; a burning was all I felt in the excitement of the time; but the hot blood flowed so fast that I soon sank to the ground and managed to crawl back from the line about five yards and could go no further from the loss of blood.

PVT. IRA BLANCHARD
20TH ILLINOIS INFANTRY

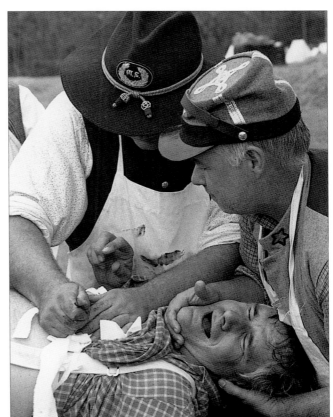

REMOVING THE BALL

Requesting the nurse to bring up his case of instruments, he said to me, "You were soldier enough to get shot; I reckon you are soldier enough to have the ball cut out." I told him that I had no choice in the matter of getting shot, but I guessed the ball would have to come out. At last he said, "Chambers, I don't like to cut there." Then as if pulling himself together, he said, "Well, turn your head away. I don't want you to look at me."

PVT. WILLIAM PITT CHAMBERS
COMPANY B, 46TH MISSISSIPPI

only a canvas tent or even just a blanket for protection, their common colds could turn into pneumonia or bronchitis in a matter of days.

Infectious diseases such as tuberculosis, smallpox, and influenza were also brought to the camps by thousands of men who should never have been in the army. Medical inspections were sporadic at best and often overlooked entirely. In their rush to fill the ranks, many recruiters and hastily formed regiments took any man who could walk and looked outwardly healthy. When medical inspections did exist, they often consisted solely of verbal questions to the recruit, with no physical examination. As a result, more than 400 women were able to bluff their way into the ranks—despite supposed medical inspections. By the end of 1862, more than 200,000 men had been discharged from the Union army as unfit, either from the ravages of disease or preexisting health problems.

The filth of the stagnant camps and lack of clean clothing also brought hordes of flies, mosquitoes, lice, and fleas, all bearing germs and disease. Hunting for "graybacks" (lice) became a daily activity, with sol-diers trying to rid themselves of the pest. Boiling their clothes or smoking them over a fire helped somewhat, but as one soldier lamented, "For every one you kill there are a thousand to take their place." But lice and fleas were a minor inconvenience compared to mosquitoes. More than a million cases of malaria decimated the Union army alone. The 38th Iowa lost 421 either killed or incapacitated by malaria out of 900 men. Soldiers referred to malaria as the "shakes" or "ague" and dreaded its sudden and mysterious onset. One soldier wrote, "Malaria, like a nightmare, settled on the camp, crushing all hope and energy out of the men." Another noted, "Morning sick call showed a rapid increase. Men were taken down sick, unfit for duty, who a few hours before felt all right; but with shivers running down the spine which later turned to fever, they would throng the doctor's tent." The only effective treatment was massive amounts of quinine, which had the side effect of loosening the teeth to the point where a soldier could not chew his rations.

The medical community blamed malaria on poisonous vapors and respiratory ailments on stale air. Medical science was still in its infancy, often more

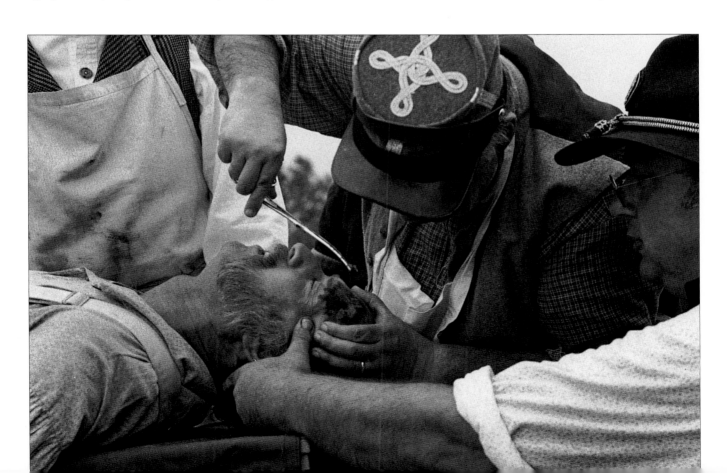

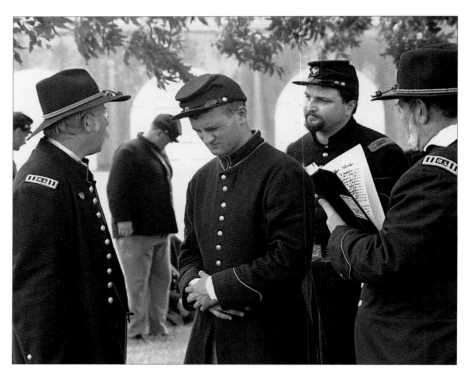

EVERY MORNING AFTER ROLL CALL, SOLDIERS WERE GIVEN THE OPPORTUNITY TO SEE THE SURGEON FOR SICK CALL. WITH NUMEROUS DISEASES AND DYSENTERY RUNNING RAMPANT THROUGH THE CAMPS, THESE LINES WERE OFTEN LONG. SOME SOLDIERS FEIGNED ILLNESS TO AVOID CAMP DUTY OR DRILL. IT WAS UP TO THE SURGEON TO DETERMINE TREATMENT AND SPOT DECEIT.

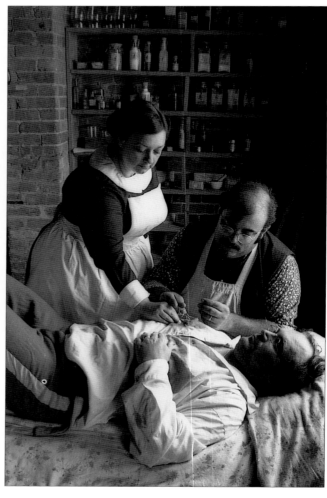

twenty large lead balls in a single shot, which could tear a group of men to pieces and cause horribly traumatic injuries. This meant that one surgeon might have dozens or even hundreds of casualties to deal with, thereby greatly increasing each man's time before treatment.

It also increased the time before a wounded man could be collected from the field, lying helpless as battle raged around him and his life's blood slipped away. In a large battle with massive casualties, a soldier could lie on the field for hours, even days—long enough for the shock to wear off and the pain to come and for infection to set in. Pvt. Richard Ackerman of the 5th New York was wounded in the thigh at the Second Battle of Bull Run. "I was wounded Saturday P.M. I laid on the battlefield for 48 hours and then rode in a government wagon for 48 hours more. Last night at one o'clock my wound was dressed for the first time." This delay in treatment proved fatal for Ackerman, who died four months later from complications.

Once a wounded man was retrieved, he was taken to a field hospital where a regimental surgeon evaluated his condition. Overwhelmed by the sheer numbers of wounded, surgeons would decide who could be saved and who couldn't. Belly and chest wounds were usually considered fatal, and these men were left to die if there were other cases to treat. The rest of the wounded were ranked by the severity of their wounds. The more serious cases were placed on an operating table—or any available platform—where the surgeon would probe the wound often with unwashed hands, simply wiping them on his bloody apron between patients.

With so many traumatic injuries—in many cases with bones shattered beyond repair—the surgeons opted for the quickest treatment: amputation. Of the 174,200 limb wounds treated by Union surgeons, 30,000 were amputations. If amputation was necessary, the patient was given chloroform, whiskey, or laudanum, if it was available, and then held down while the surgeon sawed off the shattered limb as quickly as possible. As fast as one man was removed

from the operating table or wooden board, another was put on.

If there were no broken bones, the wound would be probed until the bullet was located and extracted, either using surgical forceps or the surgeon's fingers. The wound was then dressed with nonsterilized cotton, and the soldier was taken away to await removal to a hospital by wagon, train, or boat. Since fighting armies were often far from cities, the journey often took days in overcrowded transports, and many wounds became infected long before an injured man got to a hospital.

Once at a hospital, a soldier's chance for survival improved—though not by much. Hospitals, too, were often overcrowded, with poor ventilation, bad food, and minimal hygiene. At the beginning of the war, only sixteen military hospitals existed nationwide. But as casualty figures soared, both sides built as many

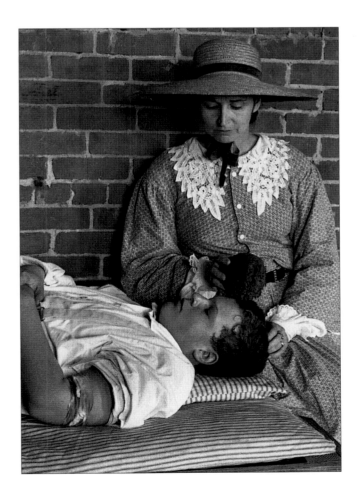

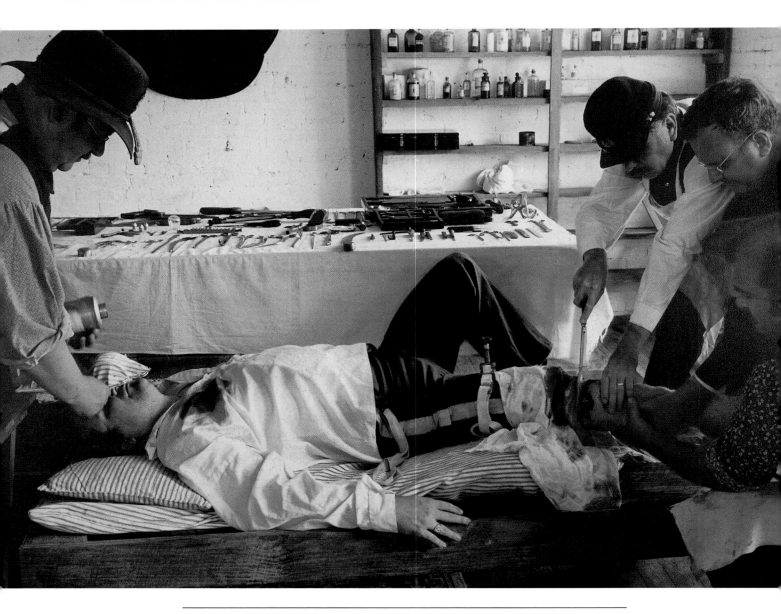

AMPUTATION

In the yard thear was 3 or 4 Large tables in it & as the soldiers was put on it (that was wounded), the surgical Corps Came along & the head of the Corps had in his hand a piece of White Chalk & he marked the place whear the Limb was to be Cut off & right behind him was the line of surgeons with thear instruments & [they] proceeded to amputate. . . . you Could see many legs Laying in the yard with the shoes & stockings on—not taken off when amputated & in a field to the left of this house was a long line of dead soldiers.

CAPT. JAMES WREN
48TH PENNSYLVANIA INFANTRY

hospitals as possible. By war's end the Union had 240 hospitals and the Confederacy had 150, including thirty-four in Richmond alone. Some of these were massive complexes, such as Chimborazo in Richmond, which had 8,000 beds and treated 77,000 patients during the war. This overcrowding made hygiene almost impossible. Bedding was used until it rotted, and bandages were washed in plain water and reused. Many of the doctors were men who were either too old or too inexperienced for field hospitals. Infection was so common that it was considered part of the healing process, and thousands died from blood poisoning or gangrene. One form of gangrene called "hospital gangrene" existed only during the Civil War. Starting as a small black spot on the wound, it would spread, rotting the flesh as it did. If the infected area was not cut out, the patient died a slow, miserable death as gangrene consumed him.

These conditions made a living hell for the wounded. Alexander Hunter wrote that the nights at the hospital were

> like the dim caverns of the catacombs, where, instead of the dead in their final rest, there were wasted figures burning with fever and raging from the agony of splintered bones, tossing restlessly from side to side, with every ill, it seemed which human flesh was heir to. From the rafters the flickering oil lamp swung mournfully, casting a ghastly light upon the scene beneath.

Not only did the wounded suffer from physical ills, but the deplorable conditions and long recovery time caused extreme depression and homesickness, which could drain a man's will to live as surely as infection.

On both sides, civilian volunteers helped the legions of wounded men by providing food, clothing, and nursing. In the North, Dr. Henry W. Bellows, a Unitarian minister, created the U.S. Sanitary Commission in 1861. His purpose was to provide an agency that "would attempt to do those things to improve life for soldiers that the government felt unable to do." Using donations, the commission

improved camp and hospital conditions throughout the army, especially through diet and medical supplies. Its efforts greatly improved soldiers' morale and their physical health. The South, with blockaded ports and dwindling supplies, had a harder time providing organized relief and depended more on local community efforts and individual volunteers, especially women.

On both sides, thousands of women worked in the hospitals and even on the battlefront, caring for the wounded. Yet the hospitals could also be dangerous for the nurses. Author Louisa May Alcott contracted typhoid fever and was treated with calomel, causing mercury poisoning that affected her health for the rest of her life. The nurses' work could also be severely depressing, leaving them feeling helpless against the overflowing tide of wounded. Clara Barton described the conditions after the Battle of the Wilderness:

> Crowded into one old sunken hotel, lying helpless upon its wet, bloody floors, five hundred fainting men hold up their cold, bloodless, dingy hands, as I passed, and beg me in Heavens name for a cracker to keep them from starving (and I had none); or to give them a cup that they might have something to drink water from, if they could get it (and I had no cup and could get none).

Despite their circumstances, the nurses worked tirelessly to aid the wounded by providing food (when available) and comfort to accelerate their recovery.

It was these acts of mercy and compassion that the soldiers valued most, providing some sense of home among the dreadful conditions the men endured, reminding them of their mothers, wives, and sweethearts. A Virginia artilleryman expressed the sentiment of all wounded soldiers in his praise of the nurses: "The ladies of Richmond, may God ever bless them, from the maiden of sixty to the young girl in her teens, moved like ministering angels among the sufferers, doing all their power to relieve the soldier's pain and suffering."

∽ CHAPTER FIVE

On the March—
Moving the Armies

Since the volunteer armies were recruited by individual states, both sides had vast manpower spread out over the countryside. To make a working army, all of these men had to be assembled in central staging areas, often hundreds of miles from their point of origin. Moving large numbers of men quickly over a long distance was usually done by train or ship. Many of the young recruits, especially those from rural areas, had never even seen, much less ridden on, a train or steamboat; to these men, this was the first adventure in their introduction to army life. Since most shipping docks and train terminals were located in large cities, it also provided many of the soldiers their first glimpse of city life—though their city experience was usually brief, since camps were located outside the towns to keep these young soldiers away from the bars, bordellos, and other activities that could consume their energy and money.

For most recruits, train or ship travel quickly lost its uniqueness—train travel was used by both armies throughout the war to move masses of troops to the battlefronts quickly. Such reinforcements could be a deciding factor in the outcome of a battle. Stonewall Jackson's brigade arrived by train at First Manassas in time to bolster the crumbling Confederate line. The Army of Northern Virginia sent 12,000 men under Gen. James Longstreet to Georgia to reinforce Gen. Braxton Bragg's army at Chickamauga and then back

to Virginia. Union troops traveled even farther since most of the fighting occurred on southern soil. For the western armies, the Mississippi River became a major thoroughfare for troops and supplies. On the eastern seaboard, the U.S. Navy transported Union troops by ocean to South Carolina, Florida, and Louisiana.

Despite the soldiers' expectations, most travel by ship or train was no joy ride. As many troops as possible were packed into the available space. On trains, this meant all types of freight and passenger cars were

---

ROUTE STEP

The march began about 7 a.m. The air was almost suffocating, and as we advanced and our canteen became empty, matters assumed a serious turn. The dust in the road was scalding and, as one person remarked, "was thirty feet deep." The soil of Virginia was sucked into our throats, sniffed into our nostrils, and flew into our eyes and ears until our most intimate friends would not have recognized us.

PVT. JOHN W. HALEY
17TH MAINE REGIMENT

used. Wilbur Fisk of the 2nd Vermont described the conditions on one winter train ride:

> The most of our brigade were crowded into open cars, that had been used for drawing coal and the floors were covered in crocky coal dust. The body of the car was a box about a foot and a half high, and into these we put our guns, our knapsacks, and ourselves. There was room enough for all of us to stand up, but not half enough for us all to be down.

Fisk and his comrades spent fourteen hours traveling in these cramped, open cars in freezing weather. Overcrowding was even more prevalent on ships. On civilian steamboats, shipmasters billed the army per man and tried to pack as many as possible aboard. (This practice caused the worst maritime disaster in American history. On April 26, 1865, the steamboat *Sultana* was transporting recently freed Union prisoners of war homeward. Overcrowded to more than twice the ship's capacity, the boilers exploded, and 1,700 men perished.)

However, once the men got to the field, soldiers on both sides quickly learned that the army had only one method of moving massive amounts of men and supplies—by marching. The Civil War soldier spent much of his time marching, trying to chase or flank the opposing army and occupy towns and territories. Sherman's march to the sea covered 1,000 miles from Georgia to South Carolina. Confederate Stonewall Jackson's brigade was known as the "Foot Cavalry" and walked 4,222 miles during the war.

On either side the routine was the same: The night before a march the camp was full of activity, with officers gathering to receive orders and arrange their regiments. Supplies were issued, with each man receiving three days' rations of hardtack and salt pork and sixty rounds of ammunition.

At 4:00 A.M. the drums sounded first roll call, and then troops were dismissed to pack gear, eat, and attend sick call. At 6:00 A.M. the men reassembled by regiment, and the march began. Union soldier David Thompson described what an army on the move

looked like: "The gathering of such a multitude is a swarm, its march a vast migration. It fills up every road leading in the same direction over a breadth of many miles."

Supply wagons were either in the center roads flanked by infantry and artillery for protection or to the rear of the troops. The troops were usually marched in columns, four abreast by brigade. The cavalry rode the outer fringes of the march, and the rear was usually brought up by ambulances and provost to pick up stragglers.

The march usually started off in good spirits—a multitude of voices talking, joking, or singing while the soldiers stepped in unison, arms at shoulder. But it didn't take long for the fatigue of marching to take its effect. Troops became silent, not wanting to waste breath in talking or singing. The march was changed to "route step," wherein each soldier set his own pace and carried his weapon however he felt comfortable. New recruits carried all their issued gear plus

GUARDING THE WAGONS

And so it goes, slow walk, then run. . . . Imagine, then the feelings of the infantry who have been detailed to guard the wagon train. Two men go with each wagon. Of course, they walk, creep, run or halt, just as the wagon they accompany walks, creeps, runs or halts, and in twelve to fifteen hours this becomes not only monotonous but maddening.

LT. THOMAS GALWEY
8TH OHIO INFANTRY

numerous personal effects, adding up to fifty pounds or more. With an average day's march covering twelve to sixteen miles, the weight of the soldier's gear seemed to increase with every step. Discarded equipment quickly lined the sides of the roads as each man tried to lighten his load to a bare minimum. Veteran regiments already stripped to the essentials would sometimes follow newer units, picking through their castoffs for resupply. Veterans learned to travel light, discarding anything they didn't use on a regular basis. A veteran's gear consisted of one set of clothes, one weapon, a haversack with food, a canteen, and a blanket and ground cloth. Each man toted a few personal items he deemed worth carrying such as a small sewing kit, a book or Bible, writing implements, playing cards, and eating utensils. Many discarded the knapsack in favor of a blanket roll because the straps of a knapsack cut into the shoulders and concentrated the weight on the upper back downward, whereas a blanket roll allowed the soldier to distribute the weight more evenly. All personal gear was placed on the spread-out blanket, which was then

rolled up and the ends tied together to form a loop. This loop was worn across the body, usually from the left shoulder to the right hip, allowing the musket to be carried or fired from the right shoulder.

Shoes were the most important item to soldiers on the march. Often ill fitting and stiff, they pinched the feet and caused blisters, turning every step into torture. Capt. William DeForest described the experience:

Oh the horrors of marching on blistered feet! Heat, hunger, and thirst are nothing compared to this torment. When you stand, you seem to

CARD GAMES

When two or three soldiers were gathered together, there did a deck of cards make its appearance among them and they proceed to exchange their meager earnings. Some gambled day and night; draw poker of course, being the game. When out of money, a man stayed in the game by resorting to the use of "O.P." ["order of the paymaster"].

ALEXANDER HUNTER
17TH VIRGINIA INFANTRY

be on red hot iron plates; when you walk, you grimace with every step. . . . The best soldiers become nearly mutinous with suffering. They snarl and swear at each other; they fling themselves down in the dust, refusing to move a step further.

Veterans learned to soak new shoes in water and let them dry on the feet, forming a tighter fit. If a blister did develop, it would be lanced with a needle threaded with wool to wick out the liquid, leaving the skin intact to form a callus rather than an open wound.

Weather and road conditions also added to the exhaustion of the troops—though there was no good weather to march in. In the winter or on rainy days, the tramping of thousands of men, horses, and wagon wheels turned roads into quagmires. Tally Simpson of the 3rd South Carolina lamented in a letter to his sister, "The mud was almost knee deep and about as thick as corn meal batter. We waded through it like horses and such a squashing you never heard. I believe I had over fifteen or twenty pounds of mud clinging to my shoes and pants." In dry weather the same tramping kicked up huge clouds of dust. Capt. Abner Small described marching "through blinding clouds of dust, hot and choky, that filled our noses and our mouths, sifted down our necks, up our trouser legs, filled our shoes, and with sweat made a cement that fastened shoes, socks, and feet together."

The heat and dust increased the soldiers' thirst and drained their energy. Army regulations suggested a break every hour, but this rarely did any good since there was no set time to do it. The army moved in fits, stopping and starting at different times. Breaks were often too short for rest but long enough for

muscles to cramp before resuming the march. Private Fiske described the effects of this interrupted pace: "Marching by rods is like dying by inches and it gets an inpatient man into a hell of a misery. . . . We rarely halted long enough to sit down, but if we did, the column would invariably start just as we were fairly seated. Men fell out, whole companies at a time." As the march continued, thirst, exhaustion, and sunstroke caused more men to fall out, and the sides of the roads were lined with debilitated soldiers. After a day's march, men straggled into the camp throughout the night.

Meager water and limited food caused many soldiers to search the countryside for supplies. A marching army expended lots of energy, and the rations of

LOST IN THOUGHT

While we awaited the order to set forward I studied with interests the physiognomies of our men. They had by this time quite lost the innocent, pacific air which characterized them when they entered the service. Hardened by exposure and suffering, they had a stoney, indifferent stare and an expression of surly patience, reminding me of bulldogs and bloodhounds held in leash. It is impossible to divine from their faces whether they expect battle or a peaceful march.

CAPT. JOHN WILLIAM DEFOREST
12TH CONNECTICUT VOLUNTEER INFANTRY

bread and salt pork were inadequate to satisfy their hunger or replenish nutrients.

The men took every opportunity to supplement their diet, whether it be from wild berries or a farmer's field. One farmer likened the passing armies to a plague of locusts stripping the land bare. Although both sides had rules against foraging, they were frequently ignored. Soldiers would claim that livestock tried to "attack" them and they killed the creature in self-defense, or it simply "wandered into the ranks" and therefore became army property. A hungry regiment could strip a farmer's field or orchard in a matter of minutes. Other property was destroyed, as well. Fences were pulled down for shelter and firewood. One soldier related that they were told to take only top rails. But as each rail was lifted off, the next one became the "top rail"—until the entire fence disappeared.

As the war continued with no end in site, foraging became a tool of warfare, especially for the Union army. The North realized that defeating the Confederacy meant destroying its source of supply as well as its army. This changed the concept of warfare forever. It became known as "total war," with the civilian population suffering as much as the armies. Food and supplies were confiscated, property looted or destroyed. The farmlands of the Shenandoh Valley were laid to waste by Sheridan's army, who boasted that "a crow flying over would have to bring his own rations." To the west, the ever-pragmatic General Sherman took this form of warfare to new heights. After taking and destroying Atlanta, he decided to march to the sea through Georgia and South Carolina and slash the South in half. To move freely, he cut his supply lines and ordered his army to live off the land. His troops destroyed anything they could not use to keep the Confederates from resupplying, and his army carved a fifty-mile-wide path of destruction from Atlanta to Charleston. Sherman swore that he would "make Georgia howl." Harsh as this new warfare was, it had the desired effect, breaking the back of the Confederacy and starving its armies into submission.

NUMEROUS AMBITIOUS CIVILIANS FOLLOWED THE ARMIES. PHOTOGRAPHY WAS INVENTED IN 1839 AND THE CIVIL WAR BECAME THE MOST PHOTOGRAPHED EVENT OF THE 19TH CENTURY. SOME PHOTOGRAPHERS, SUCH AS MATHEW BRADY AND ALEXANDER GARDNER, SAW IT AS A WAY OF DOCUMENTING HISTORY, WHILE MORE ENTERPRISING PHOTOGRAPHERS SUPPLIED SOLDIERS WITH TINTYPE AND AMBROTYPE PORTRAITS TO SEND TO THEIR LOVED ONES.

ALSO DOCUMENTING THE WAR WERE NUMEROUS JOURNALISTS AND NEWSPAPER ARTISTS. ALMOST EVERY MAJOR NEWSPAPER ON BOTH SIDES SENT CORRESPONDENTS INTO THE FIELD. TO BEST COVER THE ACTION, THESE ARTISTS AND WRITERS OFTEN WERE CLOSE TO THE BATTLE LINES. THIS ATMOSPHERE CREATED A SENSE OF CAMARADERIE AMONG THE JOURNALISTS. IN THE NORTH, THE REPORTERS REFERRED TO THEMSELVES AS "THE BOHEMIAN BRIGADE."

TROOPS ON THE MARCH OFTEN OVERREACHED THEIR SUPPLY LINES. TO SUPPLEMENT THEIR MEAGER RATIONS THEY RAIDED FARMERS' FIELDS, STOREHOUSES, AND LIVESTOCK. A LARGE ARMY COULD STRIP THE COUNTRYSIDE BARE. NO FOOD SOURCE WAS SAFE FROM THE HUNGRY SOLDIERS.

To defeat the South, the Union army had to destroy the Confederates' source of supply. Rail lines were routinely torn up. To keep the iron rails from being reused, soldiers would bend them by heating the iron track over a fire built from the wooden rail ties.

Once the rail was heated red hot, troops would grab either end and bend the rail around a tree or telegraph pole rendering the rail useless. The troops on Gen. William Sherman's march through Georgia and the Carolinas were especially proficient at this technique, and the miles of bent rails were referred to as "Sherman's Hairpins" and "Uncle Billies' Bowties."

FALLING IN FOR MARCH

Tuesday morning, camps were broken up, tents struck, knapsacks packed; and soon long lines of troops were in motion over hill and dale all around us. The roads for miles were choked with supply wagons, ammunition trains and rumbling batteries. All was noise, confusion, and utmost activity. Trumpets sounded, drums beat, whips cracked, mules squealed, and teamsters cursed. In short, all things showed that a vast army was on the move.

PVT. SAMUEL FISKE
14TH CONNECTICUT VOLUNTEERS

CHAPTER SIX

Facing the Beast—Battle

Although combat occupied only a small amount of the soldiers' time, it was, of course, a foremost concern. Before their first battle many worried whether they would stand the test or "show the yellow streak" by running. This fear of being shamed in front of their comrades kept many men in line. A sense of unity and brotherhood to their fellow soldiers made them face the danger when every instinct told them to flee. Union private John Meecham described his feelings before initial combat:

> My heart beat tumultuously. I thought I might be killed and had no wish to die. I longed to live, and thought myself a fool for voluntarily placing myself in the army. Yet I had no idea at all of turning back. My feelings were, that if ordered to go on, I would go, but gladly would have welcomed the order 'About Face.'

Waiting in reserve to go into battle was a nerve-racking experience. Still vulnerable to long-range artillery, men stood in formation, unable to protect themselves, while the sounds of warfare raged in front, often hidden from view by dense smoke. A soldier's sight of battle was often the carnage left behind by the passing armies. Elisha Stockwell of the 14th Wisconsin was introduced to the grim realities of war at the battle of Shiloh. "The first dead man I ever saw was a short distance from the clearing. He was leaning back against a big tree as if asleep, but his intestines were all over his legs and several times their natural size. I didn't look at him twice as it made me deathly sick." Troops were sometimes held in reserve near field hospitals and had to witness the pain and mutilation of the wounded, like some foreboding sign of what awaited them.

Men reacted to the stress of waiting in many ways. Some were silent, lost in thought; others joked to

---

SKIRMISH IN THE TIMBER

There was a very heavy firing to the left of the road in a chaparral of brush and scrubby pines and oaks. There the musketry was a steady roar and the cheers and yells of the fighters incessant. . . . I heard the hum of bullets as they passed over the low trees. Then I noticed that small limbs of trees were falling in a feeble shower in advance of me. It was as though an army of squirrels were at work cutting off nut and pine cone laden branches. . . . I saw a straggling line of men clad in blue . . . taking advantage of cover.

PVT. FRANK WILKERSON
NEW YORK ARTILLERY

relieve the tension. Some found solace in prayer or food; others threw away cards, dice, or pornographic pictures, worried that they might be sent home with their personal effects should they be killed.

Once they were actually in combat and felt a renewed sense of control over their actions, many men were surprised by their calmness. Union private Herbert Valentine wrote, "After the first round was fired, the fear left me and I was as cool as I ever was in my life." Others reacted by replacing fear with rage and an overwhelming urge to win; everything, including survival, became secondary to taking the enemy's position.

But many never got over their fear and carried it into every battle, reacting to orders automatically as if in a dream. Capt. James Carnahan of the 86th Indiana described how fear affected these men: "In such moments men grow pale and lose their nerve. They are hungry but cannot eat; they are tired but cannot sit down. You speak to them, and they answer as if half asleep; they laugh, but the laugh has no joy in it." For these soldiers the panic only increased once they were in combat. Their actions became confused, and they fired wildly without aiming. This was especially true of the new recruits. In the first battle of Manassas, it was estimated that 8,000 bullets were fired for every man hit. Yet this panic could strike veterans too. After the battle of Gettysburg in July 1863, nearly half of the 27,500 abandoned guns were found to have at least two unfired rounds rammed

RALLY THE TROOPS

I turned to my men as Lee was forced to the rear and reminding them of their pledges to him, and the fact that the eyes of their great leader were still upon them, I ordered "Forward!" With the fury of a cyclone, and almost with its resistless power, they rushed upon Hancocks advancing column.

GEN. JOHN GORDON, C.S.A.

HOLDING THE LINE

Cold, heat, rain, fatigue, and danger are alike disregarded, and even God himself is, for the time, forgotten. Borne along in the human current, the soldier steps over the body of his dead brother, and rushes on unheeding the imploring cries of his best friend. Men seem like devils who have wrested the instruments of wrath and destruction from the hands of the Almighty, and wield them for their mutual destruction.

CAPT. *D.U.* BARZIZA
4TH TEXAS INFANTRY

down the barrel. In panic, their owners had repeat-
edly loaded the weapons without putting on the per-
cussion caps, never actually firing a round in the
noise and confusion of the battle.

The horrors of combat numbed and calloused
some men to the sights they witnessed. One Confederate stated that he viewed a dead man with "no more
emotion than a butchered hog." Edward Schilling of
the 4th Maryland reflected, "I have seen these sights
so often that scarcely it has any more effect than the
occasional word of pity, such as 'poor fellow.'"

The Civil War was the worst time to be a soldier.
Military technology had outpaced military tactics.
The standard infantry tactic of the time was to march
massed foot soldiers two lines deep, shoulder to shoulder, in successive waves against the enemy position.

CAVALRY SERGEANT

*Anyone who has never been a soldier might ask how you
can kill your fellow man. Easy enough. There is an
intense hatred between the two armies. . . . Each army
blames the other with all its trouble. If we have a hard
march, or are exposed to the weather, it is damn the
Yankees. If it was not for them, I would be at home and
out of this trouble, and the longer the war last, the more
intense the hatred becomes. So when we have a chance to
shoot and kill, we do it without any compulsion, and the
boys in blue feel the same way about the boys in gray.*

SGT. W.H. ANDREWS
COMPANY M, 1ST GEORGIA REGULARS

REBEL YELL

The peculiarity of the rebel yell is worthy of mention, but none of the old soldiers who heard it once will ever forget it. Instead of the deep-chested manly cheer of the Union men, the rebel yell was a falsetto yelp, but though we made fun of it at first, we grew to respect it before the war was over. The yell might sound effeminate, but those who uttered it were not effeminate by any means. When the Union men charged, it was heads erect, shoulders squared and thrown back, and with a firm stride. But when the Johnnies charged, it was with a trot in a half-bent position, and although they might be met with heavy and blighting volleys, they came on with pertinacity of bulldogs, filling up the gaps and trotting on with their never-ceasing "ki-yi" until we found them face to face.

PVT. GILBERT HAYES
63RD PENNSYLVANIA INFANTRY

WOUNDED BUCKTAIL

The nervous strain was plainly visible upon all of us. All moved doggedly forward in obedience to orders, in absolute silence so far as talking was concerned. The compressed lip and set teeth showed that nerve and resolution had been summoned to the discharge of duty. A few temporarily fell out, unable to endure the nervous strain, which was simply awful.

MAJ. FREDERICK L. HITCHCOCK
132ND PENNSYLVANIA VOLUNTEERS

Once they got within one hundred yards, they would exchange volleys and then take the position by charging, relying on brute force and overwhelming numbers. This tactic had worked well with the weaponry of previous wars. The smoothbore musket was only effective to one hundred yards and artillery was usually solid shot. By the time of the Civil War, the rifled musket and conical minié ball were deadly at 500 yards, and artillery used exploding shells with a range of 1,500 yards or more. This meant troops came under fire before they ever got within charging distance.

At Fredericksburg Gen. Ambrose Burnside recklessly launched wave after wave of massed Union infantry against a fortified stone wall on Marye's Heights. Despite vastly superior numbers, the Federals were slaughtered, losing over 12,000 men, and

never got within one hundred yards of the wall. But the Confederates virtually repeated the same mistake at Gettysburg when Lee sent 15,000 men under Gen. George Pickett against the fortified Union line. Covering a mile of ground under heavy artillery fire, the decimated ranks reached the wall under withering infantry fire and actually penetrated the Union line. But they no longer had the force to hold it, and only 40 percent of the Confederates made it back to their own lines.

Soldiers and combat officers quickly saw the futility of massed charges. They would still make an assault under orders but with dread and a certain amount of fatalism. Men would pin their names to their jackets to identify their own corpse for burial. Union general John Schofield complained, "To mass troops against the fire of a covered line is simply to devote them to destruction. The greater the mass, the greater the destruction—that is all." Yet the army high command was slow to revise its tactics, and frontal assaults were made as late as 1864. In June of that year, General Grant launched a charge at Cold Harbor that cost him 7,000 casualties, most of them within the first eight minutes.

THE GRAY LINE

Such obstinate fighting I never had seen before or since. The guns were discharged so rapidly that it seemed the earth itself was in a volcanic uproar. The iron storm passed throughout ranks, mangling and tearing them to pieces. The very air seemed full of stifling smoke and fire which seemed the very pit of hell, peopled by contending demons.

PVT. SAM WATKINS
COMPANY H, 1ST TENNESSEE

WHEN THUNDER ROARS

At a given signal, the artillery begins to belch forth its horrid missiles. The air is filled with bursting, screaming, hissing death messengers. The roar is incessant. The very elements now appear to be at war, and all the thunderbolts of Heaven seemed to be turned loose from the hands of an angry and destroying God. The tough trees, survivors of a thousand storms, are broken and dismantled; huge strong horses are felled in death like so many toys and playthings; whole ranks of living, moving men are mown down by the merciless shot and shell.

CAPT. D.U. BARZIZA
4TH TEXAS INFANTRY

ACROSS CONTESTED GROUND

There is nothing that tests men's nerves more than marching up to a line of battle that is already engaged; they know they are soon to take their place on the firing line. While making the advance they can see, hear and think, but can do nothing to take their minds off the dreadful work they know is before them. Until their own battle line is formed and they are facing the front and firing their nerves are almost at the breaking point.

SGT. RICE C. BULL
123RD NEW YORK REGIMENT

When a frontal assault did succeed, and the enemy did not break, it produced some of the fiercest fighting of the war—both sides refusing to yield, firing over the breastworks into the packed mass of men, grappling for the enemy's flags, and locked into hand-to-hand combat. Confederate major Robert Stiles was in the center of such a fight. "The battle degenerated into a butchery and confused melee of brutal personal conflicts. I saw numbers of men kill each other with bayonets and the butts of muskets, and even bite each other's throats and ears and noses, rolling on the ground like wild beasts." At such moments, everything was forgotten but holding the position and keeping the regimental colors—flags were the pride of every unit and the focal point of the

enemy's fire. Casualty rates among the color guards were appalling, yet there were always volunteers for the honor of carrying the flags.

The most brutal example of hand-to-hand combat occurred at Spotsylvania Courthouse on May 12, 1864, at a site forever known as "Bloody Angle." For eighteen hours the two armies slugged it out, separated by a line of breastworks. Nothing slowed the fighting, not even a torrential rainstorm that filled the trenches with muddy water. The musket fire was so intense that large oak trees were cut in half, and bodies were piled five and six deep against the works. Neither side yielded, and the fight simply petered out around midnight when the exhausted troops could no longer continue.

CLASHING SABERS

As they approached each other, the two bodies increased their pace, until both seemed to be moving at full speed. They met with a jar, and for some moments it was impossible to distinguish friend from foe. There could only be distinctly seen the flashing of sabers in the sunlight as blows were struck and parried.

JULIAN W. HINKLEY
3RD WISCONSIN INFANTRY

DRAWING FIRE

As the slightest exposure of a man was certain to call forth a number of shots, some of the boys concluded to try the time honored dodge of holding up a dummy. So they tied a coat to a stick or ramrod, and placing a hat on it, poked it up cautiously. Pop, went the rifles! Dummy was dropped and a shout went up from the enemy. One more rebel killed! After a little Mr. Dummy looked up again, and again the rifles blazed away. The trick was played for some time before they found it out.

SGT. BERRY BENSON
1ST SOUTH CAROLINA VOLUNTEERS

Yet hand-to-hand combat was infrequent since one side would usually yield to superior fire or high casualties. This meant that the battlefront was constantly shifting over all types of terrain, making central command of an entire battlefield difficult, and tactical decisions were often made by brigade or regimental officers. In addition, the troops themselves helped change the tactics of warfare. Seasoned veterans learned to appraise the terrain and take advantage of any natural cover. To avoid the concentrated fire of a frontal assault, regiments tried to flank the enemy, striking their sides or rear. They often attempted to hide their movements by traveling through woods or parallel roads.

All of these factors added to the confusion of the battlefield, and engagements were often started when troops simply blundered into each other. In dense underbrush or tangled swamps, any semblance of troop organization or planned tactics disintegrated.

Fights turned into confused brawls in dense smoke, with regiments intermingled and the enemy hidden from view. In these conditions soldiers often fired more by sound than sight, aiming blindly at the enemy's musket fire and yelling voices. Among the sounds of exploding shells, flying bullets, and officer's commands, men vented their rage and fear with their voices. Some yelled curses or patriotic slogans; others muttered prayers or repeated names of loved ones. Screams of wounded men and horses added to the noise. Both sides also had unique battle cries to identify their own troops and intimidate the enemy. The Union troops cheered "Hurrah!" or "Huzzah!" in unison. The "rebel yell" of the Confederates was more individualistic, with each man yelling his own version. The combined voices produced a high pitched, staccato sound resembling a "Ki-yi! Ki-yi!" or "Yip-yip!" that had a chilling effect on any Union troops who heard it.

Fighting in the woods also produced another kind of horror for the soldiers. Fires were started by sparks from gunpowder and grew quickly to raging infernos in dry underbrush. Aside from producing dense smoke and general confusion, these fires consumed everything in their path—including the helpless wounded. Soldiers on both sides sometimes ceased hostilities, working together to try and save the wounded. The rapid speed and intense heat of the blazes often thwarted their efforts. One Union soldier recalled a futile attempt to save a wounded enemy at Chancellorsville. "We were trying to rescue a young fellow in gray. The fire was all around him. The last I saw of that fellow was his face. . . . His eyes were big and blue and his hair like raw silk surrounded by a wreath of fire. . . . I heard him scream, 'O Mother! O God!' It left me trembling all over like a leaf."

Even when an army won a large battle, it was rarely able to pursue the retreating foe because the chaos left the armies disorganized and physically exhausted. Discarded equipment, broken weapons, and bodies littered the shattered landscape. Soldiers with faces blackened by gunpowder, wandered the

THE HORRORS OF WAR TENDED TO MAKE MEN CALLOUS. REALIZING THAT DEAD MEN HAD NO USE FOR THEIR POSSESSIONS, SOLDIERS WOULD OFTEN TAKE THE SHOES, CLOTHING, AND FOOD OF CASUALTIES TO RESUPPLY THEIR OWN NEEDS. THIS WAS ESPECIALLY PREVALENT AMONG THE ILL-SUPPLIED AND HALF-STARVED CONFEDERATE TROOPS. NEAR THE END OF THE WAR, MANY CONFEDERATES VIEWED THE WELL-SUPPLIED UNION DEAD AS AN OPPORTUNITY TO GAIN NEW CLOTHES OR FOOD FROM THE DEAD SOLDIER'S HAVERSACK.

field seeking lost regiments and wounded comrades. Some soldiers pilfered the dead, seeking new shoes, clothing, or food. Armies often lost one-fourth of their total strength in a single battle due to casualties, prisoners, or desertions. Some regiments suffered staggering casualties, decimating them to the point that they ceased to exist as a fighting force. In the cornfield at Antietam, the 1st Texas lost 82 percent of its men. The 26th North Carolina lost 708 men out of 800 in the battle of Gettysburg. Union forces suffered as badly. The famed "Iron Brigade" comprised of 1,800 men had only 600 survivors after Gettysburg and was disbanded.

With a smaller population to draw from and limited manpower, such losses became irreplaceable for the Confederate army. This changed their tactics to a defensive position to conserve their forces and deliver

RALLY ROUND THE COLORS

As we worked our way through the woods, we stumbled upon the dead and wounded at every step; and the wounded would often cry out in their intense suffering. All night we could hear them begging for water, and occasionally one would be asked to be killed and relieved of his suffering.

PVT. JAMES DINKINS
COMPANY C, 18TH MISSISSIPPI INFANTRY

APPREHENSION

The shock to the nerves were indefinable—one stands, as it were, on the brink of eternity as he goes into action. As we thus stood listlessly, breathing a silent prayer, our hearts having ceased to pulsate or our minds on home and loved ones, expecting soon to be mangled or perhaps killed, someone makes an idiotic remark; this time it is Mangle, in a high nasal twang, with "Damned sharp skirmishing in front." There is a laugh, it is infectious, and we are once more called back to life.

CAPT. FRANK HOLSINGER
19TH U.S. COLORED INFANTRY

heavier casualties on the attacking Union army. In May and June of 1864, the Army of Northern Virginia inflicted over 77,000 casualties on Grant's forces—an even greater number than the Confederates had in the field. The Union army then revised its tactics, building defenses and besieging the Confederates, hoping to starve them out or find a weak spot in their defenses.

This created a new form of combat known as trench warfare that changed the tactics of war forever. Both sides built miles of intersecting fortified trench works, often less than 100 yards from the enemy. For weeks and even months, the stalemated armies faced each other, living in the trenches through all weather conditions. Life in the trenches was monotonous and nerve-racking. Due to sniper

HEAD TO HEAD

Our men lay piled up, one atop the other nearly all shot through the head. There were many among them I knew well, five from my own company. On the rebel side [of the works], it was even worse. In some places the men were piled four or five deep, some of whom were still alive. I have sometimes hoped, that if I must die a soldier, I should prefer to die on the battlefield, but after looking at such a scene, one cannot help turning away and saying Any death but that.

PVT. WILLIAM FISK
COMPANY E, 2ND VERMONT

THE ASSAULT

The truth is, when bullets are whacking against tree trunks and solid shot are cracking skulls like eggshells, the consuming passion in the breast of the average man is to get out of the way. Between the physical fear of going forward and the moral fear of turning back, there is a predicament of exceptional awkwardness.

PVT. DAVID L. THOMPSON
9TH NEW YORK VOLUNTEERS

DISMOUNTED TROOPERS

Every three out of the file or four sprang to the ground, committing to the lucky fourth man the charge of the horses of his file. Sabers were unbuckled, revolvers unstrapped and hung on the pommels of the saddles, leaving each trooper armed with his carbine; for this dismounting meant fighting on foot as infantry.

PVT. ALEXANDER HUNTER
17TH VIRGINIA INFANTRY

fire and occasional shelling, activities were limited, and the soldiers lived under constant threat of sudden death from the unseen enemy. The opposing trench lines were often close enough to communicate with. When not forced to fight, these opposing soldiers got along quite well. Sometimes they arranged informal truces, pledging not to fire without prior warning, and even meeting between the lines to trade food and newspapers. Yet, the soldiers knew that any truce was temporary, and at any time they might have to kill each other in combat.

Each army had gone to war expecting a few quick battles and a decisive victory. However, the bravery and determination of their troops created a stalemate, and the only way to end the conflict was to bleed the enemy dry. There was no glory in this war, only a formula for destruction.

ARTILLERY AT SUNSET

Then for seven or eight minutes ensued probably the most desperate fight ever waged between artillery and infantry at close range without a particle of cover on either side. They gave us volley after volley in front and flank, and we gave them double cannister as fast as we could load. From our second round on a gray squirrel could not have crossed that road alive.

AUGUSTUS BUELL
ARTILLERY BRIGADE, 1ST DIVISION I CORPS

CHAPTER SEVEN

Cost and Consequence— The End of the War

The casualties of battle did not end when the guns ceased firing. The wreckage of a battlefield made the landscape look like a great storm had passed over it. Dead and wounded men and horses covered the ground, lying in every conceivable position, flesh torn in every way possible. Discarded and broken equipment was everywhere. Landscapes and buildings were torn asunder, reduced to smoking ruins. John Beatty of the 3rd Ohio described the sight he saw after the battle of Murfreesboro:

> In one place a caisson and five horses are lying, the latter killed in harness and fallen together. Nationals and Confederates, young, middle aged, and old are scattered through the woods for miles. Farther on we find men with their legs shot off; one with brains scooped out with a cannon ball; another with half a face gone; another with entrails protruding. . . . Many wounded horses limping over the field. One mule, I heard of, had a leg blown off the first days of battle; next morning it was on the spot where first wounded; at night it was still standing there, not having moved an inch all day, patiently suffering, it knew not for why or for what.

The sights of carnage that the surviving soldiers witnessed would remain with them for their entire lives. As in all wars, many men found ways to rationalize their emotions and get on with their lives. For others the trauma of their war experiences would haunt them until death.

There was another direct casualty from battle, whose trial for survival began when the fighting ceased. More than 672,000 men would be captured by the enemy. In the early years of the war, prisoners were exchanged on a one-for-one basis. By 1863, however, both armies had decided that giving trained soldiers back to the enemy was a bad idea, and the exchange ceased. Numerous prisoner of war camps were hastily constructed, and 405,000 soldiers would finish the conflict within their walls. Neither side put much effort or resources toward maintaining these installations. Most Union camps were located farther north to prevent escape, and Confederates from the

---

DAWN PICKET

It rained horribly nearly all night. I got well drenched, was very cold toward morning and never but one more unpleasant night on picket. There was not a gun fired and nothing relieved the monotony of rain and darkness till daylight.

LT. CHARLES B. HAYDEN
COMPANY I, 2ND MICHIGAN

LAST RITES

Nearby I saw a handsome youngster; a Virginian, I think. I knelt beside him, and wondered if perhaps he was sleeping, he was so calm and still. He unclosed his eyes, and looked into mine with an intense questioning gaze, an appeal most beseeching, most eloquent; but I had no answer to the riddle. I asked him where he was wounded. He drew his hand slowly to his breast, and I knew there was little chance for him. I asked him if he was afraid to die. He whispered, "No, I'm glad I'm through with it." A spasm of pain closed his lids. I couldn't bear to leave him. I put my head down close to his; and suddenly he opened his eyes again; and I shall never forget their unearthly beauty, nor the sweet, trusting look that spread over all his face as he said to me, "I'm going home. Goodbye." I did weep; I couldn't help it.

MAJ. ABNER R. SMALL
3RD MAINE INFANTRY

temperate South faced long, frozen winters in drafty wooden barracks with threadbare clothes and blankets. Confederate prisons were old converted warehouses or open stockades with little shelter. In addition, the South was barely able to supply food and medicine to its own troops, and had little to spare for Yankee prisoners. Prison guards and administrators on both sides were often men unfit for other service due to injury, incompetence, or temperament. All these factors combined to make the prisoners' existence a living hell. With no activities other than roll call and meal call, time weighed heavily on the POWs, and each day was a struggle for mental and physical survival. Able-bodied prisoners tried to occupy their time with letter writing, card games, artwork, or conversation, but supplies were hard to come by, and hours were spent thinking of loved ones or their own impending fate. Some cracked under the pressure or simply lost their will to live. Lelander Cogswell of the 11th New Hampshire reflected on

the condition of his fellow captives. "The sufferings of the body were not equal to the tortures of the mind. The uncertainty as to our prospects of release, the strange isolation from the outer world . . . the gradual but sure weakening of the body—all had a depressing effect upon the mind, and finally many became insane."

Neither side was prepared for the sheer numbers of prisoners and the camps became overcrowded, unsanitary, and vermin ridden. Disease ran rampant, and food was often spoiled. The worst prison of all was Andersonville, a Confederate prison in southern Georgia, consisting of twenty-eight acres enclosed by a wooden stockade. More than 33,000 men were crowded into this area, with no shelter, polluted water, and little food or medical care. These men died at the rate of a hundred per day in the summer of 1864, with over 13,000 total deaths. By the war's end, more than 30,000 Union and 26,000 Confederates had died in the squalor of the prisons.

SAYING GOODBYE

Our company buried their dead just before sunset; and when the funeral dirge died away, and the volleys were fired over their graves, many a rugged man whose heart was steeled by years of hardship and crime, shed tears like a child, for those bound to him by such ties as make all soldiers brothers.

PVT. WILLIAM G. STEVENSON
ARMY OF NORTHERN VIRGINIA

It was not just the armies that suffered. Besides the outright destruction of property, civilian populations had to deal with the aftermath of battle. Defeated armies left behind their dead and often the seriously wounded, as well. The victors provided only rudimentary burials before moving on and left the wounded to recover in field hospitals until they could be moved. Nearby towns were stuck with the overwhelming number of dead and wounded to care for. Gettysburg, with a population of 2,400, was overwhelmed by 40,000 casualties. The wounded occupied every available building and taxed the communities' resources for weeks until the army could move them. Civilian contractors had to be hired at the rate of a dollar per body to bury the rotting corpses and burn the dead horses. The stench of death permeated the air for months.

In the South, civilians suffered even more. The North's policy of total war devastated the Confederate homefront, with property and livestock seized or destroyed. Entire cities including Charleston, Atlanta, and Richmond, were put to the torch by invading Union forces. With their homes destroyed, thousands of Southern families became refugees, fleeing the advancing armies, seeking shelter and food. The lifestyle and economy of the South was shattered, and it would take years to recover.

Slowly, the Confederate armies were worn down through starvation and attrition until surrender became the only option. When the end came, events happened in rapid succession. By April of 1865, Gen. Robert E. Lee's once proud army was reduced to fewer than 30,000 ill-equipped and hungry, ragged soldiers.

AFTER THE BATTLE

We sit on the works and let our legs dangle over on the front and watch the Johnnies carry off their dead comrades in silence but in a great hurry. Some of them lay dead within twenty feet of our works—the live Rebel looks bad enough in his old torn, ragged butternut suit, but a dead Rebel looks horrible all swelled up and black in the face. After they were through there was nothing left but stains of blood, broken and twisted guns, old hats, canteens, every one of them reminders of the death and carnage that reigned a few short hours before.

SGT. SAMUEL CLEAR
116TH PENNSYLVANIA REGIMENT

LYING IN WINDROWS

Men cover the ground in fragments, and are buried in detail, beneath the iron hail. . . . Caissons explode, and wheels and boxes strew the ground in every direction. Horses by the score are blown down by the terrible hurricane and lie shrieking in agony. . . . We open fire and men go down by scores but others fill the gap. . . . They go down like jack straws—they lie in windrows.

MAJ. ABNER SMALL
16TH MAINE REGIMENT

Many had neither shoes nor weapons and were surviving on a handful of corn a day. Surrounded by vastly superior members, Lee decided to end the bloodshed, and he surrendered his army on April 12, 1865, at Appomattox Courthouse. Two weeks later, Gen. Joseph Johnston surrendered his depleted forces to William Tecumseh Sherman in South Carolina, and on May 26 the Trans-Mississippi became the last Confederate army to surrender.

The war was over but at an enormous cost, and the consequences would be felt for generations. Financially, the war cost the North $6 billion and the South $4 billion. Much of the Confederate financing had been from European loans, which the shattered South could never pay back. Much of the southern population had been reduced to abject poverty and had to rebuild their lives from the ground up.

The true cost of the war must be measured in the millions of lives it changed. More than 600,000 men were killed and an even larger number wounded, many crippled for life. Some soldiers never fully recovered from the mental trauma of their experiences; others became addicted to drugs, hooked on the laudanum and morphine needed to quell the pain of their wounds. But each soldier was also an individual, with parents, wives, children, or sweethearts, all of whom were affected as well.

The Civil War was a tragedy of national proportions. However, good did come of it. Slavery was forever abolished, and the nation's democratic direction was redefined. Despite four years of hatred and bloodshed, the two sides were able to reunite as one nation of Americans.

The soldiers themselves helped to initiate the healing process. With the fighting over, they felt a certain kinship to their former enemies. Shared experiences and hardships created a bond that only fellow soldiers could understand. Both Grant and Sherman offered generous terms of surrender, asking only that the defeated Confederates relinquish their arms and pledge an oath of allegiance before returning home.

THE END HAS COME

. . . all hopes were gone, and the thought of returning home, defeated, seemed to be depicted on each face, and for a few days I don't think I saw a smile. . . . As for myself, I think I passed a few days of the blankest part of my existence. I seemed to have no thought of the past, present or future.

SGT. WILLIAM A. FLETCHER
TERRY'S TEXAS RANGERS

Union soldiers felt little animosity toward their former foes and often a sense of respect for their valor and pity at their loss. When Lee's troops surrendered at Appomattox, there was no cheering from the assembled Union troops, only an awed silence. Union soldiers went to "Present Arms" as a salute to their former foes, watching with sympathy as these ragged, defeated men stacked weapons and furled their flags for the last time. When the ceremony was over, they came forward to offer these hungry rebels rations from their own haversacks.

For most Union soldiers the prominent emotion was a sense of relief that it was finally over. They had accomplished their task and survived. "Never shall I forget the feeling that passed over my soul just before retiring," wrote a Union cavalryman. "The knowledge that now we could go to bed and feel sure of enjoying a full night's rest." Many simply wanted to go home and forget the horrors they had experienced. Illinois surgeon John Hostetter expressed the sentiment of many war-weary soldiers: "There is no God in war. It is merciless, cruel, vindictive, unchristian, savage, and relentless. It is all the devils could wish for."

For the Confederate soldier an overwhelming sense of despair superseded his relief. Years of bloody sacrifice had come only to defeat. Many wept openly as they surrendered, or they walked around in a daze, unable to comprehend their defeat. "My God! That I

should have lived to see this day! That I hoped I should die before this day," wrote one Confederate. With much of their homeland in ruins, others tried to comprehend their future. Sgt. James Whitehorne of the 12th Virginia reflected on his last day as a soldier: "The war has been going on for so long I can't realize what a man would do now that it is over. How can we get interested in farming or working in a store or warehouse when we have been interested day and night for years in keeping alive, whipping the invaders, and preparing for the next fight?" Some Confederates refused to surrender and live under Yankee rule. Over 10,000 fled to foreign countries, although most eventually returned to their homeland.

Many soldiers felt a sadness when the regiments disbanded and comrades went their separate ways. A brotherhood had been formed that would stay with them all their lives. As the years passed and the terror of their experiences faded, many of these former soldiers felt a certain nostalgia for their time in the army.

For many their war experience was the defining moment in their lives that only other soldiers could comprehend. Both sides formed veterans organizations that met year after year to share their memories. The Civil War had changed America forever. These old soldiers wanted their descendants to understand the sacrifice they had made, and veterans from both sides helped heal the country's wounds by working together to erect monuments and establish national parks and cemeteries. They also worked to develop a pension plan for soldiers and their widows.

In 1913 a few surviving veterans met at Gettysburg to commemorate the fiftieth anniversary of the battle. These former adversaries shook hands over the stone wall where they had fought so long before. As the years passed, these old warriors finally passed away, leaving behind a legacy of American determination and a belief that the ideals of freedom were worth more than anything else—including life itself. Now the veterans of this great war are once more with their comrades, once more resting in long orderly rows under the marble tombstones, lying in cemeteries built to honor their sacrifice.

NEVER GOING HOME

"I have, I know, but few and small claims upon Divine Providence, but something whispers to me—perhaps it is the wafted prayer of my little Edgar, that I shall return to my loved ones unharmed. If I do not my dear Sarah, never forget how much I love you, and when my last breath escapes me on the battle field, it will whisper your name. Forgive my many faults, and the many pains I have caused you. How thoughtless and foolish I have often times been! How gladly would I wash out with my tears every little spot upon your happiness.

But, O Sarah! If the dead can come back to this earth and flit unseen around those they loved, I shall always be near you; In the gladdest days and in the darkest nights. . . always, always, and if there be a soft breeze upon your cheek, it shall be my breath, as the cool air fans your throbbing temple, it shall be my spirit passing by. Sarah do not mourn me dead; think I am gone and wait for thee, for we shall meet again.

MAJ. SULLIVAN BALLOU
2ND RHODE ISLAND
(KILLED, FIRST MANASSAS)

✑ Bibliography

EYEWITNESS ACCOUNTS

Andrews, W. H. *Footprints of a Regiment*. Atlanta: Longstreet Press, 1992.

Ayers, James T. *The Civil War Diary of James T. Ayers*. Edited by John Hope Franklin. Springfield: Illinois State Historical Society, 1947.

Beatty, John. *Memoirs of a Volunteer*. Edited by Harvey S. Ford. New York: W. W. Norton, 1946.

Benson, Berry. *Confederate Scout-Sniper*. Edited by Susan Williams Benson. Athens: University of Georgia Press, 1992.

Billings, John D. *Hardtack and Coffee*. 1887. Reprint, Alexandria, VA: Time-Life Books, 1982.

Blackford, Susan Leigh. *Letters From Lee's Army*. Edited by Charles Minor Blackford. New York: A. S. Barnes, 1947.

Blanchard, Ira. *I Marched With Sherman*. San Francisco: J. D. Huff, 1992.

Brown, Robert Carson, ed. *The Sherman Brigade Marches South*. Washington: Charles Brown, 1977.

Bull, Rice C. *Soldiering: The Civil War Diary of Rice C. Bull*. Edited by K. Jack Bauer. Novato, CA: Presidio Press, 1977.

Chambers, William Pitt. *Blood and Sacrifice*. Edited by Richard Baumgartner. Huntington, WV: Blue Acorn Press, 1994.

Chisholm, Daniel. *The Civil War Notebook Of Daniel Chisholm*. Edited by W. Springer Menger and J. August Shimrak. New York: Ballantine Books, 1989.

Dawson, Francis W. *Reminiscences of Confederate Service*. Edited by Bell I. Wiley. Baton Rouge: Louisiana State University Press, 1980.

Deforest, John William. *A Volunteer's Adventures*. New Haven, CT: Yale University Press, 1974.

Dinkins, James. *1861–1865: Personal Recollections and Experiences in the Confederate Army by an Old Johnnie*. Edited by Kenneth Bandy. Dayton, OH: Morningside Bookshop, 1975.

Fisk, Wilbur. *Hard Marching Every Day*. Edited by Emil and Ruth Rosenblatt. Lawrence: University of Kansas Press, 1983.

Fletcher, William A. *A Rebel Private: Front and Rear*. New York: Penguin Books, 1975.

Forbes, Edwin. *A Civil War Artist at the Front*. Edited by William Forrest Dawson. New York: Oxford University Press, 1957.

Gardner, Alexander. *Gardner's Photographic Sketchbook of the Civil War*. 1866. Reprint, New York: Dover Books, 1959.

Haley, John W. *The Rebel Yell and the Yankee Hurrah*. Edited by Ruth L. Silliker. Camden, ME: Down East Books, 1985.

Haskell, Frank and William C. Oates. *Gettysburg*. Edited by Paul Andrew Hutton. New York: Bantam Books, 1992.

Hayden, Charles B. *For Country, Cause, And Leader*. Edited by Stephen W. Sears. New York: Ticknor and Fields, 1993.

Higgins, Thomas Wentworth. *Army Life in a Black Regiment*. New York: Collier Books, 1962.

Hitchcock, Frederick L. *War from the Inside*. 1904. Reprint, Alexandria, VA: Time-Life Books, 1981.

Holmes, Oliver Wendell. *Touched by Fire*. Edited by Mark DeWolf Howe. Cambridge, MA: Harvard University Press, 1946.

Jackman, John S. *Diary of a Confederate Soldier*. Edited by William C. Davis. Columbia: University of South Carolina Press, 1990.

McCarthy, Carlton. *Detailed Minutiae of Soldier Life.* 1882. Reprint, Alexandria, VA: Time-Life Books, 1982.

McClenen, Bailey George. *I Saw The Elephant.* Edited by Norman E. Rourke. Shippensburg, PA: White Mane Publishing, 1995.

Pettit, Frederick. *Infantryman Pettit.* Edited by William Gavin. New York: Avon Books, 1990.

Poague, William Thomas. *Gunner with Stonewall.* Wilmington, NC: Broadfoot Publishing, 1987.

Ranson, John L. *John Ransom's Diary.* New York: Dell Publishing, 1963.

Rhodes, Elisha Hunt. *All for the Union.* Edited by Robert Hunt Rhodes. New York: Orion Books, 1985.

Roberson, Elizabeth Whitley, ed. *In Care of Yellow River.* Gretna, LA: Pelican Publishing, 1997.

Schilling, Edward. *My Three Years in the Volunteer Army of the United States of America, 1862–1865.* Edited by Barbara Schilling Everstine. Baltimore: 1985.

Sillman, Justus M. *A New Canaan Private in the Civil War.* Edited by Edward Marcus. New Canaan, CT: New Canaan Historical Society, 1984.

Simpson, Tally and Dick Simpson. *Far, Far From Home.* Edited by Guy R. Everson and Edward W. Simpson. New York: Oxford University Press, 1994.

Small, Abner R. *The Road To Richmond.* Edited by Harold Adams Small. Los Angeles: University of California Press, 1959.

Smith, Benjamin T. *Private Smith's Journal.* Edited by Clyde C. Walton. Chicago: R.R. Donnelley and Sons, 1963.

Stevens, George T. *Three Years In The Sixth Corps.* 1866. Reprint, Alexandria, VA: Time-Life Books, 1984.

Stockwell, Elisha Jr. *Private Elisha Stockwell Jr. Sees the Civil War.* Edited by Bryon Abernathy. Oklahoma City: University of Oklahoma Press, 1958.

Watkins, Sam R. *Co. Aytch.* New York: Collier Books, 1962.

Wills, Charles W. *Army Life Of An Illinois Soldier.* Carbondale, IL: Southern Illinois University Press, 1996.

Worsham, John H. *One Of Jackson's Foot Cavalry.* Edited by Paul Andrew Hutton. 1912. Reprint, New York: Bantam Books, 1992.

Wren, James. *Captain James Wren's Civil War Diary.* Edited by John Michael Priest. New York: Berkeley Books, 1990.

EYEWITNESS ACCOUNT COMPILATIONS

Abell, Sam and Brian Pohanka. *Distant Thunder.* Charlottesville: Thomasson-Grant, 1988.

Cannan, John, ed. *Eyewitness History of the Civil War: War In The East.* New York: Gallery Books, 1990.

———. *Eyewitness History of the Civil War: War In The West.* New York: Gallery Books, 1990.

Coco, Gregory A. *The Civil War Infantryman.* Gettysburg, PA: Thomas Publications, 1996.

Commager, Henry Steele, ed. *The Blue and the Gray.* New York: Fairfax Press, 1960.

Congdon, Don, ed. *Combat: The Civil War: The Climactic Years.* New York: Dell Publishing, 1967.

Cotton, Gordon A., ed. *Yankee Bullets, Rebel Rations.* Vicksburg, MS: Office Supply Company, 1989.

Davis, William C., ed. *Brothers in Arms.* New York: Gallery Books, 1995.

Denny, Robert. *The Civil War Years.* New York: Sterling Publishing, 1992.

Eisenscimil, Otto and Ralph Newman, eds. *The Civil War: An American Iliad.* New York: Mallard Press, 1956.

Gates, Betsey, ed. *The Colton Letters, 1861–1865.* Scottsdale, AZ: McLane Publications, 1993.

Gragg, Rod, ed. *The Illustrated Confederate Reader.* New York: Harper and Row Publishing, 1989.

Holzer, Harold, ed. *Witness To War: The Civil War, 1861–1865.* New York: Berkeley Publishing Group, 1996.

Johnson, Robert Underwood and Clarence C. Buel, eds. *Battles and Leaders of the Civil War.* New York: Thomas Yoseloff, 1956.

Katcher, Phillip. *The Civil War Sourcebook*. New York: Facts On File, 1992.

Meltzer, Milton, ed. *Voices from the Civil War*. New York: Harper Collins, 1989.

Miers, Earl Schenk and Richard Brown, eds. *Gettysburg*. New Brunswick, NJ: Rutgers University Press, 1948.

Miers, Earl Schenck. *The General Who Marched to Hell*. New York: Collier Books, 1965.

Nofi, Albert A., ed. *Eyewitness History of the Civil War: The Bloody Struggle*. New York: Gallery Books, 1988.

————. *Eyewitness of the Civil War: The Opening Guns*. New York: Gallery Books, 1988.

Poe, Clarence, ed. *True Tales of the South at War*. 1961. Reprint, New York: Dover Books, 1995.

Robertson, James I., Jr., ed. *Soldiers Blue and Gray*. Columbia: University of South Carolina Press, 1988.

Straubing, Harold Elk, ed. *The Fateful Lightning: Civil War Eyewitness Reports*. New York: Paragon House Publishers, 1985.

Tapert, Annette, ed. *The Brothers' War*. New York: Vintage Book, 1988.

Wheeler, Richard, ed. *Voices of the Civil War*. New York: Meridian Books, 1990.

Williams, Hermann Warner Jr., ed. *The Civil War: The Artist's Record*. Boston: Beacon Press, 1961.

GENERAL REFERENCE

Catton, Bruce. *Glory Road*. New York: Doubleday Books, 1952.

————. *Never Call Retreat*. New York: Doubleday Books, 1965.

————. *Reflections on the Civil War*. New York: Doubleday Books, 1981.

————. *A Stillness At Appomattox*. New York: Doubleday Books, 1953.

————. *Terrible Swift Sword*. New York: Doubleday Books, 1963.

————. *This Hallowed Ground*. New York: Doubleday Books, 1956.

Davis, William C. *Fighting Men of the Civil War*. New York: Gallery Books, 1989.

————. and Bell I. Wiley. *Photographic History of the Civil War*. 2 vols. New York: Black Dog and Leventhal Publishers, 1994.

Donald, David, ed. *Divided We Fought, 1861–1865*. New York: Macmillan, 1952.

Foote, Shelby. *The Civil War*. 3 vols. New York: Random House, 1963.

Linderman, Gerald F. *Embattled Courage*. New York: Collier MacMillian, 1987.

Lord, Francis. *They Fought for the Union*. New York: Bonanza Books, 1960.

Lowry, Thomas P., M.D. *The Story The Soldiers Wouldn't Tell: Sex in the Civil War*. Mechanicsburg, PA: Stackpole Books, 1994.

Miller, Francis Trevlyan, ed. *The Photographic History of the Civil War*. 10 vols. New York: Castle Books, 1957.

Mitchell, Reid. *The Vacant Chair*. New York: Oxford University Press, 1993.

————. *Civil War Soldiers*. New York: Penguin Books, 1988.

Robertson, James I., Jr. *Tenting Tonight: The Soldiers Life*. Alexandria, VA: Time-Life Books, 1984.

Time-Life Books, eds. *Echoes Of Glory: Arms and Equipment of the Confederacy*. 3 vols. Alexandria, VA: Time-Life Books, 1991.

Ward, Geoffrey C. *The Civil War*. New York: Alfred Knopf Books, 1990.

Wiley, Bell Irvin. *The Life of Johnny Reb*. 1943. Reprint, Baton Rouge: Louisiana State University Press, 1970.

Wiley, Bell Irvin. *The Life of Billy Yank*. 1943. Reprint, Baton Rouge: Louisiana State University Press, 1970.